Only Believe

**An Eyewitness Account of the Great
Healing Revivals of the 20th Century**

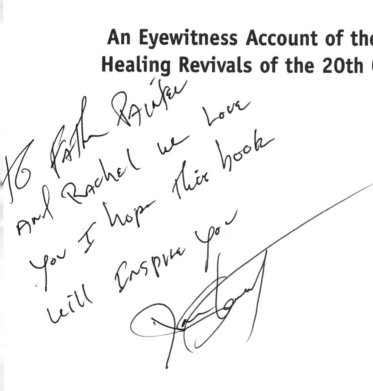

Only Believe

An Eyewitness Account of the Great
Healing Revivals of the 20th Century

Don Stewart

The interviewer, as designated by bold type, is Doug Wead, who graciously helped the author prepare this book.

Photographic images on the front cover are used by permission of Roberts Liardon Ministries Inc.

Revival Press

An Imprint of
Destiny Image® **Publishers, Inc.**
P.O. Box 310
Shippensburg, PA 17257-0310

ISBN 1-56043-340-X

For Worldwide Distribution
Printed in the U.S.A.

This book and all other Destiny Image, Revival Press, and Treasure House books are available at Christian bookstores and distributors worldwide.

For a U.S. bookstore nearest you, call **1-800-722-6774**.
For more information on foreign distributors, call **717-532-3040**.
Or reach us on the Internet: **http://www.reapernet.com**

Dedication

To the three "Brens" in my life, who are the result of the grace of God—the God of second chances:

My loving wife, Brenda, who is my best friend and companion. Life simply works better with her by my side.

My miracle son, Brendon, who was born because Brenda stood on the promise of Psalm 37:4: "Delight thyself also in the Lord; and He shall give thee the desires of thine heart."

My darling daughter, Brenna, "Daddy's girl," who is my princess and my joy.

The greatest treasures can be found in a man's own home.

Acknowledgments

Special thanks to all those who provided hands, feet, and wings to my journey:

To Doug Wead, who encouraged me to write this book, patiently walked me through the memories, and asked the probing questions that drew out the facts.

To my long-time friend and associate, Bob Daniels, who helped with research and numerous rewrites.

To Pastor Rob Thompson, who read the first draft and offered constructive suggestions.

To Rev. Sven Blomberg and Rev. Buford Dowell, who helped jog my thoughts to recall some of the details that had slipped my recollection.

To my long-time associate, Larry MacKay, for his reliable insight and wisdom. And to his wife, Joy, my secretary, who typed tirelessly on the multiplied drafts of this volume.

To Don Nori, Jr., Elizabeth, and the editors at Revival Press whose diligent guidance and direction were vital in the creation of this book.

To all my "spiritual children" all over the world who constantly remind me of God's power to heal and perform miracles. If I were ever tempted to doubt, the testimonies they share with me of how they were healed and blessed under my ministry—many of them years ago—continually convince me of the life-changing grace and mercy of God.

And, of course, to my spiritual father and mentor, the late Rev. A.A. Allen, who believed in me when no one else did. Without his influence, this book could never have become a reality.

Endorsements

"Don Stewart gives here a very candid, eyewitness account of life behind the scenes and on the platform of one of the greatest moves of God: the healing revival of the 1940's and 50's. Sharing from his life working alongside A.A. Allen and his interactions with other ministers who operated in incredible giftings from God, he brings forth an understanding about the lives and the times—the good and the bad; the trials and the triumphs—of these faith greats. Herein are the stories, insights, and wisdom from someone who was there on the front lines of that move of God."

—Roberts Liardon
Author and Pastor

"I've known Don Stewart for more than 15 years and consider him to be one of the most kind, loving, and caring individuals I know. As I have had the privilege of previewing *Only Believe*, faith as a giant was awakened within me. To recount the stories of the great men of God of recent generations, reminded me of how the children of Israel were told by Moses to continually put the works of God before their children's eyes. May your life be greatly enriched because of this wonderful work Don Stewart has put together."

Robb Thompson
Senior Pastor
Midwest Christian Center

"No one I know has spun so well a yarn of historical and traditional insight into the great healing revival of the mid-twentieth century, as Don Stewart."

—Rt. Rev. Dr. W. Nah Dixon
President of Liberian Council of Churches
Monrovia, Liberia, West Africa

"*Only Believe* is an insider's view of the healing revival. Don Stewart gives a perspective that cannot be reached through research only. He was a part of it. You will be fascinated by the history of the movement."

—Bishop Don Meares
President and Founder of International Congress of Local Churches
Pastor of Evangel Church, Washington, D.C.

"*Only Believe* takes us through the electrifying history of the 'Faith Healing' ministries of the twentieth century, through the eyes and ears of one of its most significant protagonists. Don Stewart tells us how God has used him and others in this most amazing and controversial ministry. All those who need healing, or who just want to learn more about the power of the Holy Spirit, need to read this book."

—Rich Wilkerson
Evangelist
Founder and President of Peacemakers International
Pastor of Trinity Church, North Miami, Florida

"Don Stewart's compelling boldness as a healing evangelist jumps out at you as he brings forth God's healing power in this anthology of the most celebrated faith healers. You will cry for joy as the blind see and the lame walk. *Only Believe* will take you on a journey through God's ever loving mercy and grace as they are depicted through visible healings."

—John Godzich
Evangelist, Author, and Businessman

"In Don Stewart's book, *Only Believe,* he opens our eyes to the fact that God is still in the miracle business. Since Jesus Christ is the same yesterday, today, and forever, our faith has been stimulated to believe the Lord for even greater miracles today.

"As we examine the miracles of the past, it encourages us to 'only believe' that all things are possible in these last days. Thank you, Don, for encouraging us to 'only believe' and trust in the Lord with all our hearts."

—Pastor Dennis Leonard
Heritage Christian Center
Denver, Colorado

Contents

A Word From the Author

When I was asked to write this book, the opportunity was instantly exhilarating. Revisiting and reliving some of the great moments in legendary ministries was a possibility I could revel in with no difficulty.

It wasn't long before I found myself swimming in an ocean of mixed emotions and encountering a small struggle with hesitation. This volume was not to be the usual narrative format. The challenge presented to me was to answer direct questions from an interviewer of no minor stature or experience. Doug Wead is a gifted writer and scholar, and he is certainly not anyone's "yes man." He would be thorough and tough. Evasive "uhs" and "ers" would not be acceptable. I was bidden to come clean with an honest assessment of all areas of inquiry.

My earliest training under my mentor, Rev. A.A. Allen, directed me never to be critical or judgmental of other ministers or ministries. This has been my goal in response to each question presented in this book. Talents and gifts of various kinds are given by God to willing servants. Who are we to question or condemn the wisdom and purpose of God?

The first disciples called to follow Jesus came from a variety of backgrounds and abilities. They were an eclectic mix of fishermen, a doctor, a tax collector, and so on. Each had his own way of doing things. This was reflected in their individual ministries. They had different styles and expressions—even different opinions about some of the things the Master taught them.

Yet, they were united through mutual dedication to the commission of lifting up their Lord as the Savior and Healer of mankind. They were eager and open channels for the public demonstration of God's power and purpose in the world. Here, their hearts beat as one.

That's pretty much the picture of the ministries discussed in this book. They are valid expressions, varied and different in style and method, yet joined together by a sacred commitment to honor the name of God through their calling and gifts.

These are unique individuals of yesterday and today. They are brothers and sisters in the Lord devoted to the highest calling known to mankind: the preaching of the gospel of Jesus Christ with power and demonstration through the Holy Spirit.

My intent on these pages is not a finger-pointing, whisper-behind-the-back kind of book. It's not an exposé or a "tell all" scandal sheet. (That might be a disappointment to some readers.) I make no attempt to glamorize, sanitize, or eulogize any of the personalities presented here. My comments and observations are honest, straightforward opinions based on personal knowledge, recollections, and research. My hope is to provide some informative insight into one of the most fascinating and controversial eras of contemporary Church history.

—Don Stewart

Introduction

All Things Are Possible

I was a youngster when I first sat under the ministry of William Branham. It seemed like the whole world had gathered at that fairgrounds in that small town in southern Indiana. At the time, Branham didn't preach at his own crusades. He was much too shy and, by his own admission, too uneducated for that. Of course, it only added to the mystique and the maddening anticipation. "When is he going to show? Is he really here? I heard that he wasn't coming."

For the past year, Branham, a humble, Indiana, Baptist preacher, had been conducting his crusades up and down the West Coast. In Oregon and Washington he had begun to draw huge crowds. Auditoriums weren't holding the numbers. Supposedly, remarkable things were happening. People were claiming healings. Some were calling him the new Aimee Semple McPherson or Charles Price.

The Assemblies of God, the largest Pentecostal denomination in the country, was being bombarded with mail. "Who is this guy? Is he doctrinally sound? Is he a fraud? Can we co-operate with his meetings?"

In those days, my father was the point man for the Assemblies of God in Indiana. He was called the District Superintendent, which meant he was sort of the denomination's bishop for the state. "What do you know about a Baptist preacher named William Branham?" Headquarters asked. Dad had never heard of him. "Well, he's from your state, so check him out."

Every Sunday my father spoke in a different Assemblies of God church somewhere in the state. It was a time of unprecedented growth.

In Indiana they opened a new church every month, a pace that would continue for 12 straight years. Traveling the state was Dad's way of trouble-shooting the District problems and promoting the statewide events. There were four boys in the family and on this particular weekend, I was elected to go with Dad.

At first glance, William Branham was not a very impressive guy. It looked like he had slept in his suit. No one even introduced him. After the sermon and the altar call, he just wandered up to the microphone. His first words were an apology for his poor English. But the crowd apparently knew what was coming. When they realized it was him they broke into a roar of conversation, drowning out his voice, and then there was a belated but spontaneous and excited applause. In those days, people never applauded in church. But they had been waiting all afternoon for this moment.

And then Branham pointed up to my father. "The man up there. No, not you. The man to your right. No, not you. The one behind you. The one in the blue suit."

My father sunk lower and lower in his seat. No one knew he was going to this meeting. The General Superintendent of the Assemblies of God didn't know. Mom didn't know. Dad himself didn't know until that morning when his host pastor had dropped the news that Branham was conducting a Sunday afternoon service nearby.

My father had been surprised. As far as he had known, Branham was still ministering in the Pacific Northwest. Dad hadn't even told the pastor what he was up to. But now William Branham was calling him out of the audience.

Dad looked at me solemnly. "Now, you stay right here," he ordered. "Whatever happens, stay right here. I'll be back."

According to my father, as he related the story in later years, Branham welcomed him to the platform, pulled him aside, and said, "You and I have never met. I don't who you are or where you come from. But I saw you in a dream last night and I knew you would be here today. God sent you here to confirm my ministry. You may ask any question you want. You may talk to any of the people in the healing line. You may interrupt what is going on at any point. You do what God tells you to do. You are here to confirm my ministry."

Over the next few years my father did just that. At some meetings he rearranged the healing lines, just in case Branham was only invoking some parlor trick, memorizing who had what disease. He quizzed the people who claimed that they were healed, taking down names and addresses. And often he would call their doctors to talk about what had happened. On more than one occasion he would spot a friend from out of state and spontaneously walk that friend to the front of the line. But Branham would never miss a beat. "You are from Iowa," he would say. "Three weeks ago you were told by your doctor that you have cancer."

Afterwards, the friend would confide to my father, "Nobody knew that but my wife and I, and she is back in Iowa. I haven't even told my children."

Eventually, my father reported back to the General Superintendent of the Assemblies of God. But his report was rejected. Understandably, because of his own belief, Dad became a champion of the healing ministry. He was the chairman for Oral Robert's crusades in Indianapolis, Fort Wayne, and South Bend. When the Assemblies of God went to war with the *Voice of Healing*, my father stood on the floor of the national convention to defend them. He was booed and hooted down.

But the Assemblies pastors must have liked his spunk. Two years later he was elected to their national executive board where over the years he used his position to urge the denomination to be tolerant and to bring people in, not kick them out. Long after the healing evangelists were excluded from Assemblies of God churches, the Indiana District Camp Meetings continued to feature their ministries...Richard Vinyard, Velmer Gardner, Eddie Barg. Dad also traveled to Brazil with Clifton Erickson. He became a close friend to Morris Cerullo, and eventually he followed Lester Sumrall as the pastor of the great church in South Bend, Indiana.

When a gifted but controversial evangelist named Leroy Jenkins first appeared, Dad invited him to his church and tried to help give his ministry a good start. And later, as the charismatic renewal exploded on the South Bend, Notre Dame Campus, Dad was there to lend a helping hand. He raised the money to help launch the new Catholic ministry in Ann Arbor, Michigan.

He was much more patient with the ministries that others easily rejected. When Dale Zink, Indiana District Secretary-Treasurer, decided that God was calling him to work with the controversial evangelist A.A. Allen, my Dad gave his blessing. Of course, I remember well the colorful A.A. Allen. His radio program was broadcast from the high wattage, super stations across the Mexican border. These booming broadcast signals dominated the night sky, even as far north as Indiana.

And so it was almost like revisiting my childhood to sit down with Don Stewart, A.A. Allen's successor, and explore the boundaries of what had happened in those remarkable years. Stewart was a young man when he stepped into Allen's shoes, but he had survived as the last of a breed, the last true link to the great revival that swept the country in the late 1940's and 50's. In those years there was a tent and a healing evangelist on every corner. There were dozens of Benny Hinns. If you didn't like the way one preached or conducted his services, you could go to another.

I have often wondered about what I saw and heard as an innocent youngster. How would it look to me now? Was it real? Was it phony? Was it all formulas? Were the people really healed? And of what? And how? Why did some so-called "men of God" or "women of God" die of apparent drug overdoses or as alcoholics? And where did all the others go? How did it change forms? How did it metamorphose into the charismatic renewal and the Word of Faith movement and into dozens of institutions ranging from Oral Roberts University to the Full Gospel Business Men International to Christ for the Nations?

Most of all, where would it go now? Would it die with Benny Hinn? Would it be passed on to someone else? Would it break out again as it had in that decade long ago?

If there were answers to those questions, they surely lay with Don Stewart. His evangelistic association was practically a museum with hundreds of old films and magazines. There were many of the original publications of the various ministries, with some transferred to microfilm. Don's knowledge of the people and events was remarkable. He personally knew most of the major players. His understanding of the natural—the human part—of the faith healing business was invaluable. And he had personally experienced what many called "a supernatural ministry" of his own. This was his life's work. He knew as much or more about the great healing revival of the mid-twentieth century as anyone still living.

There was a new song they used to sing in those William Branham meetings. Today it is old, worn-out, and dusty, but at the time it was fresh and the people could never get enough of it. Its gentle rhythm rose and fell across the audience, mingling with the scent of the cheap Aqua Velva aftershave and the body odor that had come from hours of nervous waiting. Its soft melody was a contrast to the earlier panic...the jostling and struggling to get into the building before the fire marshal ordered the doors closed. The fight was over. They had won. They were inside. They could relax. And as they sang, a peace settled over them.

The lyrics were the words of Jesus and they offered promise to a mass of people who had come expectantly, hoping to be transported heavenward from the poverty and dreariness of their lives. They were hoping to see their daughter's crossed eyes straighten—or maybe it would happen for someone else's daughter. Some were there as a last resort. They had been given a death sentence of cancer. There was a miracle just ahead or there was nothing.

"Only believe," they would softly sing. The beginning of the service might still be hours away. There would be no song leader to coach them, no one on the platform to give them instruction, but as they relaxed and waited they would spontaneously and reverently sing the words, over and over. "Only believe. All things are possible. Only believe."

During the months of interviews with Don Stewart, that old melody sometimes came back to me. It became the background music to the many stories that he related. "All things are possible. Only believe."

–Doug Wead
Gold Canyon, Arizona

Chapter One

The Beginning of a Movement

John Alexander Dowie and Smith Wigglesworth

Is it real? Are people really healed? And can it be proved?

Yes. People are really healed. No, it can't be proved. That is to say that skeptics can offer a rationale for anything. They can say that the cancer would have gone into remission anyway or that the healing is an example of the power of "mind over matter." In Jesus' day, the religious leaders finally concluded that His healings were happening but that they were being done through the power of satan. People will generally look for any explanation other than God.

I guess the explanation that comes to my mind is that of a "misdiagnosis." That is, that the person may not have really had cancer in the first place.

That is sometimes the conclusion of a critical journalist or skeptic, but there are thousands of cases that defy such an explanation. There are the cases with before and after X-rays, for example. Sometimes the journalists themselves provide the evidence.

The story of Cathy Williams comes to mind. Cathy was a beautiful, young 15-year-old high school majorette from Savannah, Georgia. She was a good student and very popular. Then suddenly her world went dark. Doctors said that she was struck with "chronic retinal deterioration." Within months, she was totally blind in one eye and had only 80 percent use of the other. By the end of the year, they expected her to lose all sight in the good eye as well.

In this case, her story was written up in the *Savannah Evening Press*. It was a very public event. The continuing saga moved people. There were letters to the editor, and radio talk shows covered it. Money was raised for her to travel to John Hopkins University in Baltimore, Maryland. At the time there was no known cure for this problem, but the doctors at John Hopkins had agreed to examine her anyway.

Now, Cathy's family attended St. Michael's Catholic Church in Savannah Beach, and they were deeply religious. The mother had read my magazine and listened to radio broadcasts. She had been praying that I would visit the area. Well, God answered that mother's prayer. We held a crusade in Savannah. Cathy and her family came, and that 15-year-old was instantly healed. There was no charge of misdiagnosis. The whole community had known of her disease.

She was healed instantly? Just like that?

Instantly. I prayed for her and then put a handkerchief over the one eye that still had partial vision. I asked her what she could see through that blind eye, and she screamed, "I can see you! I'm healed! I can see you!"

She grabbed me and hugged me. Her mother started sobbing like a little child. Her boyfriend ran up from the audience saying, "Cathy, can you see me? Cathy, can you see me?"

"Yes," she said. She was crying and screaming. "I can see you clearly. I can see! I can see!"

The three of them hugged each other and jumped up and down with joy. Then the young man fell down on his knees and starting praying out loud in front of the whole audience. "Oh God, I'm sorry I ever doubted You. I'm going to serve You the rest of my life." It was quite a moment.

And it is all documented?

Yes. It's all there for anyone to examine.

Where did it start? How do the Christian faith healers of the twentieth century trace their roots?

Most of them would trace their doctrinal roots back to the Bible itself. That's what we would all like to believe, and that is the claim.

There is a very famous story in Exodus when Moses held up a bronzed serpent in the wilderness and all who looked at it were healed. That was part of the covenant with the Israeli people. If they would keep His commandments, He would heal their diseases. (See Numbers 21:6-9.)

The early Israeli prophets also had gifts of healing. There is the story of Naaman, the Prime Minister of Syria, who sought out the prophet Elijah to be healed of leprosy. The prophet must have had quite a reputation as a healer for the news to have reached that far north, and then to that level of society. (See Second Kings 5.)

The disciples and others in the early Church experienced such gifts, and really, all through the ages there have been periodic manifestations, specific times and places, or specific persons through which the miracles of healing would take place. St. Martins of Tours, St. Bernard, and Francis of Assisi are some who come to mind. For long periods of time, the belief in supernatural healing was the normative experience in the Church.

And yet, eventually, it disappeared?

Not entirely. And that's an important point. A slender thread of it has always remained throughout the history of Christianity. In fact, from a doctrinal standpoint, the Eastern church has consistently made room for the mystical and the miraculous, even if there have not been massive waves of spiritual revival to showcase it.

Even in the West where, yes, it was practically extinguished, individual believers continued to have occasional experiences of personal healing. Actually, Catholic doctrine allows for the *Sacrament of Healing*, though sadly, over the years the practice became know as the *Last Rites*, since the people usually died anyway. Still, there have been those moments. No matter how man has changed, God has remained the same and His compassion and power have always been able to find expression.

But the modern manifestation of healing, just how and where did it all begin?

In the United States there was the experience of the Quakers. George Fox, the founder of that religious group, left behind a *Book of Miracles* that documented some of the more famous healings in his ministry. Healing was also part of the early experience of the Adventists in this country, as well as the Churches of the Brethren. The first Latter Days Saints shared the belief in miracles of healing, and Joseph Smith referred to many stories of such.

I suppose the most celebrated early spokesman for the movement was a Scotsman by the name of John Alexander Dowie. Just about the time of the American Civil War, Dowie and his family moved to Australia. It was there that he would develop his ideas on healing. Dowie was very young at the time, just a teenager, and he was very ill. As is the case of a great many of the healing evangelists who would follow, it was only after he experienced a personal healing himself that he began to develop an interest in the subject and eventually move on to preach the message to others.

Actually, that's your own story.

Yes, and it's the story of William Branham, Oral Roberts, A.A. Allen, and many, many others. It is really a very pronounced pattern. Most of the healing evangelists of the twentieth century were first healed themselves, often of a life-threatening disease.

Well, anyway, Dowie went back to Scotland to study at Edinburgh University. During that time he began to read and hear about the ministry of Edward Irving, pastor of the National Scottish Church in Regent Square, London. Irving was openly preaching the message of divine healing, suggesting that the only reason the modern Church was not experiencing such healings was because congregations were not being told to expect God to heal. Dowie was impressed. He read every pamphlet and sermon Edward Irving published.

When John Dowie returned to Australia, he entered the ministry as a Congregationalist pastor. Now, it was one thing for the established and respected Edward Irving to proclaim the message of divine healing from his prestigious pulpit at Regent's Square in London. He could get away with it. It had shock value. It was controversial. But it was taken in the context of a long and respected ministerial career. It was something altogether different for a young Congregationalist pastor, just arriving in a new land, to preach and promote the same message. For the time being, John Dowie had to keep his theology of healing to himself. But the time would soon come for him to speak up.

Now, there was a great public issue at the time, one that dominated the debate between religious and secular societies, much as abortion does today, and that was the issue of legalized alcohol. The *temperance movement* was gaining momentum, and it was threatening to shut down the alcohol industry. As in the case of abortion, it soon became an issue of worldwide debate.

It's hard to believe that the temperance movement was that powerful. After all, alcohol was not a life-and-death issue as can be argued in the case of abortion.

Oh, yes it was. Proponents had studies showing the death rate due to alcoholism and its relationship to crime and to divorce. In fact, today, science pretty much confirms the *temperance* argument of the nineteenth century and takes it even a step further.

A huge amount of money was at stake—billions of dollars—not to mention the amount of power and influence involved. The religious world was aroused, and organizing, and going to the ballot boxes of America, Australia, and the United Kingdom. People were getting voted in or out of office over the issue. The secular and religious worlds were on a collision course.

As a pastor, John Dowie was frustrated, feeling that this great issue was passing him by. He finally decided to run for the Australian Parliament, but he was defeated. The newspapers savagely trashed him.

A few years later, still licking his wounds from his brief foray into politics, Dowie began to turn away from public life and focus on spiritual things. Soon, he launched a healing ministry, and almost immediately the crowds were too big for church buildings. Within a short time, Dowie was ministering to thousands of people in vast open-air meetings, and eventually, this ministry took him to the United States.

What kind of reception did he get here? Obviously, he was not preaching divine healing in the Congregationalist denomination?

No. By then he was an independent, faith healing preacher. Remember, this was all very, very controversial, although there was always an audience because there were always sick people who were suffering and who had no other hope.

But how could thousands of people just suddenly accept such a doctrine?

They accepted it because of the miracles. There was just no other way. People are not stupid. They can't be talked into something that defies their own logic. But when they, or someone they know personally, experiences a miracle, well then, everything changes. Dowie had some very remarkable and celebrated healings, some of which were reported in the newspapers. A congressman's wife was healed. Abraham Lincoln's cousin, who was a very prominent university president, also claimed a healing.

Actually, human nature hasn't changed as much as we would like to believe. Miracles and healings were just as shocking in biblical times. It was not the teachings of Jesus that attracted the crowds; it was the healings. It was the same for us in the 1950's. When there were miracles and answers to prayer, the word spread and the crowds grew.

And yet, there was very clear teaching in some of the churches that the day of miracles, the dispensation, if you will, was over. Practices such as Dowie's were heretical.

It's interesting that no matter what people's doctrine teaches, when they or someone they love is dying or suffering, there is almost an instinct that takes over and tells them that God loves them and that He will hear their prayer. When a father holds his sick little girl in his arms, try to tell him that God cannot or will not respond. Tell him that healing is not doctrinally correct. If he believes in God at all, then in that moment he will understand the doctrine of healing.

So Dowie was attracting people from the mainstream Protestant churches?

People came from every denomination. And the word spread. He held meetings up and down the West Coast. He found himself on the front pages of various newspapers, and he finally ended up in Chicago, holding meetings in a small wooden auditorium right at the entrance to the World's Fair. Actually, Dowie had a better location than Buffalo Bill's Wild West Show, which competed with him from across the street.

At first, the city tried to ignore him. But after several difficult months there were several miracles, and word got around. Eventually there was standing room only, with crowds outside. Now, remember, this was a very international crowd. The World's Fair was a big deal in those days. So, inevitably, some of the healings began to happen to people visiting from different countries, who then carried the news back home. The international press was intrigued.

All this infuriated the city fathers. It was an embarrassment. Chicago was becoming known around the world as a center for "faith healing." A local newspaper publisher and some of the city fathers began meeting regularly, trying to figure out a way to drive Dowie out of town. Of course, Chicago was very corrupt then—everything was for sale.

Look it up. John Dowie was arrested 100 times in 1885. It was pure harassment, of course. Local law enforcement people and judges were bribed. He was found guilty of all sorts of things. The newspapers smeared and ridiculed him.

There were unbelievable stories. His congregation took in converted prostitutes and gave them a new start, which infuriated the local organized crime bosses. But the newspapers tried to convince their readers that Dowie was running his converted prostitutes back out onto the streets to make money. It was outrageous. The local postmaster yanked his second class postage permit. Actually, there is a very eerie similarity between the Jim Bakker story where Charlotte, North Carolina's publisher and city fathers went after him. It was a nightmare, but in this case, John Dowie beat them.

How did Dowie do that?

He moved the debate out of Chicago. For example, he always appealed his court cases to the next level where they were inevitably overturned. He took his debate with the postmaster to Washington, D.C. where bureaucrats were fascinated by this larger than life character and were totally unimpressed with the threats of the Chicago publisher. Eventually, President McKinley himself got involved. Actually, Dowie and McKinley met together at the White House twice, and Dowie later met with Teddy Roosevelt.

Remarkably, within two years, the Chicago publisher was himself the target of corruption charges and actually ended up in the Joliet penitentiary. So it wasn't an easy time. But eventually, John Dowie prevailed and his meetings grew.

When one thinks of John Dowie, one thinks of the Zion, Illinois, community.

Yes, that's what most people remember, the city he built, but actually, that came later. First, Dowie moved to the very center of Chicago. His big headquarters building was right across the street from the Illinois Central Depot. It was a combination healing center, hotel, and office building. Services were held in a tabernacle on the corner of Madison and 16th Street. I think the Tabernacle is long gone, but the big hotel office building was still standing in the 1960's.

It was during this time that he announced that he would be building a new Christian community, a city, a place where Christians could live and work and play together without "worldly distractions." He actually got a British factory to move in and offer employment for some of the people. His new Zion Tabernacle, built right on the grounds, could seat 8,000 people, and it was usually full.

Of course, Dowie got a lot of criticism for this new experiment. And he was a fighter. He loved confrontation and used negative publicity to fill his auditorium. The problem was that he not only fought with the press and the politicians, but also with everybody else, even those who agreed with him. At least, that is the widely accepted story.

There were supposedly doctrinal controversies.

It didn't happen all at once. It was very gradual, but over time, things began to get out of hand. First, Dowie announced that the new city would not be a representative democracy. He declared that such a form of government was not biblical, and therefore, the city would be a theocracy. Dowie was soon running everything. Critics were calling it a cult.

Then he announced plans to build other Zion communities around the world and to eventually generate enough money to buy up land around the Holy sites in Jerusalem and build a city of Zion there. Within time, he came to believe that his new Zion of Jerusalem would, in fact, be the New Jerusalem prophesied in the Bible. He saw himself as preparing the way for the return of Christ.

The story that I remember was Dowie's claim to be the Old Testament prophet Elijah.

Well, that was the great controversy. Actually, much earlier in his Chicago ministry, a group came to him suggesting that he was the prophet Elijah come back. At the time he wisely rebuked them. But apparently the idea haunted him. Interestingly enough, the same thing happened to Bill Branham years later.

Why Elijah? Where does that idea come from?

Do you remember the Bible story of Elijah? He didn't die, but was carried away to Heaven in a fiery chariot. Well, writers and prophets in both the Old and New Testaments write about the "last days" before God's judgment of the earth, and they write about Elijah the prophet returning to earth to complete his ministry. (See Malachi 4:5 and Mark 9:11-13.)

Was it fraudulent? Was Dowie just putting people on?

Oh, no. If you read his writings you realize that he slowly began to flirt with the idea and then became firmly convinced that he was indeed the prophet. There was no money in it for him. Far from benefiting him in some way, it eventually ruined his ministry.

How does something like that happen?

Pride. It is quite a heady experience to have thousands of people reaching out just trying to touch you. At his height Dowie filled Madison Square Garden in New York City. No preacher had ever done that before. But contrary to many writings on the subject, it wasn't the doctrinal controversies alone that brought down the Zion community; it was primarily economics. Toward the end, Dowie went on a world tour to promote Zion, and in his absence there was a power struggle. Nothing was the same after that. Many of Dowie's greatest supporters turned on him.

Where did they all go? What happened to them?

Many became part of a newly formed "fellowship" called the Assemblies of God. Of course today the Assemblies of God is considered a somewhat formal, traditional Pentecostal denomination. Others joined the Apostolic churches and became part of the Oneness movement, which is yet another story.

It seems as if the life of John Alexander Dowie set a pattern. When you look at the lives of the twentieth century faith healing evangelists, all the elements are there in Dowie's story.

In some respects that's true. Almost all the great healing evangelists were controversial like Dowie. They almost all had international ministries at a time in which world travel was very, very rare. They were always on the defensive, so they tended to have combative personalities, thriving on negative publicity that invariably filled their auditoriums. And, like Dowie, they were often independent of the traditional Church, which tended to fight against them. This rejection was probably due to the threat of losing members and money to them.

But in other respects John Alexander Dowie was unique. No one who followed had the satisfaction of such a thorough public vindication of the slanders against them and their teaching. And, with the exception of Bill Branham and the claim that he was "Elijah returned," none of the faith healers ventured so far away from mainstream Protestant doctrine. Socially, they were shut outside and had no fellowship with the mainstream church, yet perhaps chastised by Dowie's sad ending, they were warned and stayed on the edges, never venturing very far away.

There was something else. Evangelists who came later constantly traveled from place to place. If someone claimed a healing and later denied it or decided that he had only been carried away by the emotion of the moment, the evangelist was long gone and could not be blamed. Dowie had to live with what he said and did. In that respect, he was a forerunner to the ministries of Aimee Semple McPherson in Los Angeles, and later, Kathryn Kuhlman in Pittsburgh. He stayed in one place. You could find him. And the people who claimed miracles of healing could be found too. They had names and addresses, medical records, family members, and doctors who were witnesses to all that had happened.

Visitors who came to Dowie's Zion Tabernacle were immediately struck by the crutches and other paraphernalia of the infirmed and sick that were hung all over the walls. These were Dowie's trophies, but they were more than that. They were symbolic of the personal testimonies of individuals who still lived in Chicago and actually worshiped at the church, persons who were readily available to prove and help document what had happened to them. This was not a con game or some deception. "Here I am. Those are my old crutches up there on the wall. Here is my doctor's address."

In the 1950's, an American evangelist, Clifton Erickson, learned how to inspire faith in a crowd by bringing forward the best examples of proven healings. He had some mammoth crusades in South America, and the miracles he was able to document really rocked the country. Later, Kathryn Kuhlman did the same thing through her books.

Did any of these ministries trace a direct link to Dowie?

Not really. The parents of Gordon Lindsay, who was to become the great chronicler of the modern healing movement, actually attended some of Dowie's meetings, and their son, Gordon Lindsay, was born in Zion, Illinois, but he himself had no other direct link. But, of course, the later ministries had heard the stories. They knew what happened.

The interesting thing is this. John Alexander Dowie finally died in 1907. That same year, thousands of miles away, an English plumber by the name of Smith Wigglesworth experienced what Pentecostals referred to as the *baptism of the Holy Spirit*, and he immediately embarked on a healing ministry that would encompass the world.

That same year in Ingersoll, Ontario, Canada, a Pentecostal evangelist held meetings in which a young lady was to have a life-changing experience and commit herself to Christ. She would later burst onto the scene as the famous evangelist Aimee Semple McPherson.

And that same year, Kathryn Kuhlman was born.

Throughout their lifetimes both Smith Wigglesworth and Aimee Semple McPherson pointed to 1907 as their beginning, though neither one spoke of John Alexander Dowie or had any link to him. As far as that goes, neither one had a link to the other. Still, there are those who see a spiritual connection. John Dowie died, and that same year, Kathryn Kuhlman was born and two other champions of God's healing power were raised up.

Smith Wigglesworth came first?

He was much older than Aimee Semple McPherson—I think there was a 30-year difference—and they ministered in different places around the world. To my knowledge, they never crossed paths.

Smith Wigglesworth was born in the United Kingdom to a family of extreme poverty. He was put to work at the age of six. By the next year, he was working 12-hour days in a mill. This, of course, was before the English child labor laws.

As is the pattern, he experienced a personal healing that eventually launched his ministry. Wigglesworth had married a young woman preacher with the Salvation Army, and even though he was running his own plumbing business, he actively assisted her work in a small mission. Curiously, they had both heard about the Pentecostal movement and had personally embraced the doctrine of divine healing. They even taught it from the pulpit of their small mission.

On a Sunday afternoon, right in the middle of an open-air meeting, Wigglesworth collapsed. He was rushed home to where an attending physician diagnosed a ruptured appendix. The doctor said that Wigglesworth was too weak to have an operation and practically gave him up for dead, saying that he would come back tomorrow to see if anything could be done then.

His wife called for some friends to pray with her, including local Pentecostals.

Wigglesworth felt the power of God go through his body. He immediately got up and asked his wife if there had been any calls for work. She reluctantly passed on some of the messages he had received from his plumbing business. Smith got dressed and walked out the door. He never had another problem. The doctor was flabbergasted.

For a time, he continued his work as a plumber, assisting his wife at the nearby mission where they both rather timidly prayed for the sick.

Then in 1907, when he was already in his late forties, Wigglesworth experienced the baptism in the Holy Spirit. After that, everything changed. His preaching was bold, even shocking. Miracles started happening. Almost immediately, he launched a worldwide ministry.

It's hard to understand how things can happen so fast.

Well, it is really a testimony to the authenticity of the healings and the answers to prayer. There were crowds overnight because some people really got answers and their enthusiasm spread. Everyone wanted him to come to their city. Within a couple of years he was traveling all over the world.

Remember this was all word of mouth. There was no television, and Wigglesworth was a plumber anyway. He had no special public relations skills. The explosive way his ministry suddenly took off suggests a spontaneous enthusiasm rather than careful promotion.

It really is a remarkable story. Wigglesworth was not a very educated man. His roots were in a poor, working-class, English family. By some accounts, he couldn't even read until his adult years when his wife taught him. In that respect, he was like the rough, working-class healing evangelists of the 1950's. Clifton Erickson was a truck driver, for example. Nevertheless, great miracles attended the Smith Wigglesworth meetings. The anticipation of his meetings was palpable. Crowds gathered long before a service would begin, and the stories would spread from one town to the next.

What were some of the stories?

Most of them were about great miracles of healing. I remember reading an account of one of the early experiences. In a nearby village a young man was dying, and his friends were begging Wigglesworth to come and pray. He finally got there, only to be told by the mother that it was too late. Her son's heart was failing. He was already a skeleton and was expected to die within the next couple of days.

Wigglesworth went into the room, saw this living skeleton that was barely breathing, and fell to his knees. He fasted and prayed all through the day and night, keeping the family out of the room. The next day he got up and went out into a nearby field to continue praying, when he suddenly saw a vision. He returned to the house to announce that God had told him the young man would be healed the next day. The family was ordered to wash his clothes and lay them out by the fireplace to dry. By this time the news that Smith Wigglesworth was in town had spread throughout the village. Some came to scoff. Others just waited outside the house to see what would happen.

On the following day, Wigglesworth again sent the family out of the room and knelt down by the frail young body. "When I touch you," Wigglesworth told the man, "God's power is going to come all over you. It will be nothing like you or even I have ever seen before. Don't be afraid. This is all happening to bring glory to God."

He prayed for another hour or so, and then he laid hands on the boy. Instantly the young man rolled over in his bed and began weeping. Wigglesworth, overcome by the power of God, fell over on the floor. He felt God telling him to stay where he was. The young man's bed started shaking. His frail voice began to chant, "For Your glory, God, for Your glory." And then, this skeleton stood up and started walking around the room.

Eventually, Wigglesworth got back onto his feet, and the two of them just stood there praising God. Well, the family was waiting in the kitchen, and they could hear all that was going on. When Wigglesworth finally opened the door, the young man called out, "Dad, I've been healed." With that, the power of God swept into the kitchen and the father fell on the floor. The mother, filled with joy, started toward her son, and then she too fell over.

Well, the whole village was shaken. Many were converted. They begged the plumber to stay and use the local Anglican church building to conduct services, but Wigglesworth kept moving. When you compound that story thousands of times, you can see how he started filling auditoriums. The legends and testimonies were spreading faster than any public relations effort could ever have done.

Actually, under the Smith Wigglesworth ministry, there were several stories of people being raised from the dead. Of course, today, there are all kinds of stories and best-selling books about people who have died in a hospital bed and been brought back. Paramedics have lots of stories about people who have stopped breathing and lost their heartbeat and still revived. There is so much new medical technology. But to talk about people being raised from the dead in funeral homes or at a wake in the 1900's, well, that is something else.

How did the established churches react?

It was very curious. Those clergymen who actually witnessed the miracles or had people in their congregation who had been healed could not easily doubt what had happened. In some cases, Wigglesworth was invited to preach for Anglican, Methodist, Salvation Army, and other evangelical congregations. Of course, the Pentecostal churches welcomed him. But among the hierarchy and career churchmen, he was very controversial. And I suppose they felt threatened by him and his ministry: *Who is this ignorant, uneducated man? How can he teach us anything?* Even some Pentecostal leaders attacked him.

What was their concern?

He was accused of being pretty tough on the people who came for healing. Of course, Jack Coe and A. A. Allen would later be taken to task for the same reason. They were always yanking people up out of wheelchairs, twisting people's necks to see if there was any pain, or practically knocking them over when they laid their hands on them. Here in the United States, the general superintendent of the Assemblies of God during some of those years was E.S. Williams, and he was one of many who were critical of Wigglesworth.

But there were no financial improprieties or weird doctrines that accompanied Wigglesworth's ministry? Not even in the latter years?

No. There was nothing like that—no scandals. Maybe Smith Wigglesworth's humble beginnings helped him keep his perspective. Maybe it was his prayer life; he prayed many hours at a time.

Before he died in 1947, Wigglesworth had traveled all over the world, throughout Asia, Africa, Australia, and across America, speaking to hundreds of thousands. His ministry was characterized by bold, uncompromising faith in God. There were thousands and thousands of converts and thousands of personal stories of healings and miracles. In a Smith Wigglesworth meeting, the impossible could happen.

By the time he died, the great healing revival of the mid-twentieth century was finally born. Smith Wigglesworth was one of the forerunners, and none would come after him with any greater ministry.

Chapter Two

Women of Faith

Maria Woodworth-Etter,
Aimee Semple McPherson, and Others

Most of my interviews with Don Stewart took place at his 30,000-square-foot evangelistic association headquarters. We would gather in his office suite and be surrounded by mountains of old magazines and flyers, many of which dated back to the 1920's. Sometimes, in response to a question, Don would buzz a staff member and ask for other materials to be brought up from his extensive archives. Sometimes he would simply pull a book off of a nearby shelf.

Invariably, at the end of the day, I was sent packing with a suitcase full of research material, including hours of old film that had been transferred to videotape. And I always came back with even more questions.

On one such occasion, I asked to review the Stewart Ministry's files on the famous woman evangelist, Aimee Semple McPherson. My own grandmother, Willa J. Short, had often served as a guest evangelist at the famous Angelus Temple in California, and I was curious to see if I could find her name in Don Stewart's

archives. So I spent a few days perusing the files and viewing the videos. My grandmother was not there. But the next time we met, Don Stewart was full of stories about the curious and prominent role of women in the great healing revival. And I was full of questions.

Perhaps the most fascinating chapter of the history of faith healing in America was written by a long line of colorful, flamboyant women evangelists. Today, the women's movement largely ignores these stories, acting as if women in the pulpit was some new phenomena that had been championed by political liberals. In fact, as you very well know from the stories of your grandmother, Willa Short, many of the early faith healing women evangelists were preaching to auditoriums of 20,000 and were routinely featured on the front pages of the nation's newspapers. The first radio sermon was preached by a woman evangelist, and it was a woman evangelist who bought the first religious radio station in America. It was an exciting time, and of course, it was very controversial.

Where did they come from?

Some of them came right out of Zion, Illinois, and the John Dowie experience. "The Mothers of Zion," they were sometimes called. Several of the women seemed to have extraordinary gifts of healing. Most of them didn't really aspire to be preachers, but the role just sort of evolved for them.

One of the more famous and mysterious who comes to mind was Martha Wayne Roberson. She didn't travel or hold crusades or publish a magazine or go on the radio. She simply prayed for the sick, but there were extraordinary miracles and the word spread. She would wake up in the morning with people waiting outside her door.

It was really quite a phenomenon. Here was this mystical old woman, who spent most of her waking moments in prayer, and she was very difficult to find, which, of course, made her all the more alluring. The attraction to her went on for years, totally driven by word of mouth. Thousands of people came and went and among them were many women who started their own ministries

Carrie Judd came out of the Roberson experience. She was a founding member of the Christian Missionary Alliance. From Carrie Judd's ministry came Dr. Gray. Then came Mary Elizabeth, who recently died at 90 years of age. For years and years, she had been one of the leaders of the "Faith Home" in Zion.

You spoke of this as a "controversial time," and yet one gets the impression that women preachers were much more accepted than they are today.

That may be the impression, and that is what most of the historians of the revival contend. Yet those who interviewed the women themselves got a very different picture. For one thing, all the Protestant churches of that time were much more conservative and fundamentalist than they are today. Modernism and the new German theology had hit the seminaries, but to the rank and file Protestant believer, the inspiration of the Bible was not questioned. There were New Testament scriptures that said that women should be silent in the church, and although some biblical scholars explained that this was in reference to the unique worship arrangement of the Jews in which women were segregated from the men in balconies and often disrupted the meeting to talk to their husbands on the floor of the synagogues, others weren't quite so sure of what the scriptures meant. This was not a time to take chances.

It's true that because of *Woman's Suffrage* and the newfound right to vote, some persons were more open to women preachers. Many started appearing during the rise of the holiness movement. The Nazarenes started to ordain women. But there is another side to the coin. The holiness revival was essentially a Methodist affair. At the time, the Methodist Church was the nation's largest denomination, and it was being shaken to its foundations. Members were trying to recapture the ardor and spirit of the original revivals of John Wesley, which had launched Methodism. New denominations were being formed. There was a new call to "holiness," separating oneself solely to God. Some felt that the best way to do this was to exactly replicate all Wesley's teachings. That included a wide range of restrictions on women. They were to be modest and to wear hats in public. Their dresses were to have sleeves reaching clear to the wrist and hems to the floors. Showing the ankle was considered risqué.

This was not an easy atmosphere for a woman to step into the pulpit. And remember, there was no precedent. Yes, there had been some precedent for healing evangelists throughout the centuries; a slender thread, I called it. But where was the precedent for Christian women leaders? The Catholic church had never ordained them. There was no woman among the 12 apostles.

In 1857, when 13-year-old Maria Woodworth-Etter announced at her moment of conversion that God had just called her to preach, well, it was just not accepted. Someone had made a mistake, and it was probably Maria. Women couldn't even vote. How could they presume to teach men about important spiritual and eternal issues?

Woodworth-Etter was the first one?

There were hundreds, many with very great ministries. I mentioned the famous Carrie Judd, who has been the subject of several books. There was Maria Burgess Brown who founded Glad Tidings Tabernacle in New York City and so many more. But Maria Woodworth-Etter was certainly one of the earliest and most respected. Her rise to national popularity was extremely unlikely, not only because she was a woman but because of her extreme poverty and lack of education. At 12 years of age, her father died. At that point in her life the woman we would come to know as Maria Woodworth-Etter had to give up any personal ambition, drop out of school, and go to work to help her mother feed the family.

It was the year after her father died that Woodworth-Etter had her conversion experience. They had been attending the Christian Church in Lisbon, Ohio, and that summer an itinerant evangelist had passed through town. During a time of prayer, Maria not only made her commitment to Christ, but she came away with an unmistakable call to preach. Her denomination, the Christian Church, had no history of women preachers at all. None.

At an early age, she married P.H. Woodworth, and they had six children. Her unlikely call to the ministry receded. Then Woodworth-Etter and her family experienced one disaster after another. One of the children died, and then a second. Eventually, five of them were lost to childhood illnesses. Some have speculated that it was in the depths of this pain that she began to search and study the Scriptures about divine healing and to formulate her ideas. In any case, relatively late in life, at age 35, she finally fulfilled her youthful calling and launched into the ministry.

How did one launch into the ministry in those days? Who would dare ordain a woman minister? How did Maria Woodworth-Etter get started?

That's a good question, and again, to answer it one has to consider the context of the times. I talked to you about the great revival that was spreading across America. The churches in all the Christian denominations routinely held special meetings or "revivals." There was a tremendous hunger, and as a result, there was a tremendous demand for evangelists.

Also remember there was no radio or television. People had to see something to believe it. Public meetings were much more common. This applied to entertainment as well. For example, there were hundreds of traveling circuses. With the advent of radio, television, and motion pictures, these circuses eventually declined in popularity, disappearing one by one until all that was left were the three big ones, the Ringling Brothers, the Barnum Circus, and the Bailey Circus. And finally, those three merged into one.

So at the turn of the century, people were in the habit of attending public meetings of all kinds. Some people would come to a revival meeting just out of curiosity. The unchurched would be especially drawn to the novelty of a woman preacher who believed in the doctrines of divine healing.

Were there big crowds?

Not at first. For the first five years, she traveled and spoke mostly in the holiness movement. She was especially popular among members of the Winebrenner Church of God. Now, this gets complex. There are actually more that 200 denominations in this country who use the words Church of God in some way or another. Most of them were born out of the Methodist holiness revival. Today, the three largest are the Church of God with headquarters in Anderson, Indiana, the Pentecostal denomination with headquarters in Cleveland, Tennessee, and the large, Black denomination, the Church of God in Christ.

So, when did she get her big break?

In January 1895, she held a meeting in Hartford City, Indiana, and the crowds swelled into the thousands. Several times they moved to bigger buildings. Then they finally moved outside into the open air.

There was a lot of emotion and excitement in her meetings. Sometimes, when the anointing was on her, people near her would just fall over. It was called being "slain in the Spirit." There were also trances. She herself would often go into a trance for hours at a time. She encouraged believers to "wait on the Holy Spirit to receive power," just as the early Church had done after the Ascension of Christ. Well, thousands of people sought this "power," claiming that they too had experienced a trance.

This had to be pretty controversial. If people were offended with a scholar like John Dowie, they must have been outraged by a woman preacher.

Yes, there were problems. More than 20 journalists came to Hartford City, including a reporter from the *New York Times*. But remember, John Dowie had stayed in Chicago. Woodworth-Etter kept moving. And eventually, unlike Dowie, she had developed a broad base of support. Before her ministry ended, the Pentecostal churches had begun to organize, and she became a beloved elder sister to them.

But yes, there was persecution. She was arrested on several occasions. Two doctors in St. Louis tried to have her declared insane and committed to an institution. The newspapers were scurrilous, alternating between sarcastic ridicule and claims of hypnotism and suggestion.

As would be the pattern for evangelists who would follow, this criticism only swelled the crowds with the curious. She was off and running. The same year of the Hartford City revival, more than 25,000 came to her meeting in Alexandria, Indiana. Eventually, she bought an 8,000-seat tent, which she took across the country. It was always packed.

She had a unique name, Woodworth-Etter.

Late in her ministry she and her husband became divorced. In fact, she charged him with adultery. He died the next year, and she became remarried with Samuel Etter. As I understand it, Maria came up with the idea to keep both surnames. And it may have had something to do with marketing, for want of a better word. She was already a national figure in the Church, known as Maria Woodworth. Yet, it was unthinkable not to take her new husband's name. Rather than start all over with a new name, she simply hyphenated it. The combining of surnames was a precedent that Aimee Semple McPherson would copy.

How did it end? Were there any scandals or charges of false doctrine?

Well, she didn't claim to be Elijah, if that's what you mean. But at the time, her doctrines and the very idea of a woman preacher were all pretty scandalous in and of themselves.

Oh, there was one incident that almost spelled disaster for her ministry. Right in the middle of one of her meetings she went into a trance, and after coming out of it, she claimed that God had shown her a disaster of biblical proportions. She claimed that there would be a massive earthquake in San Francisco. Such a pointed and specific prophecy was a little too much for many of her followers, and when nothing happened in San Francisco, Woodworth-Etter's ministry began to fade. Like any popular or successful personality, she had enemies, and they were quick to jump on this one "mistake" to discount her whole ministry.

Then, the unthinkable happened. A few years after her prophecy, on April 18, 1906, San Francisco was shaken by one of the worst earthquakes in recorded history. Fires raged across the city. Her prophecy had become a reality.

She ministered well into her seventies and eventually founded a church in Indianapolis, which exists to this day as Lakeview Christian Center.

Talk to me about Aimee Semple McPherson. I've reviewed some of the materials you gave me. Hers is a fascinating story.

Aimee Semple McPherson arguably had the greatest impact of any woman religious leader in the twentieth century. She literally left a denomination in her wake—and not just a denomination, but one that has stood the test of time, one that has consistently turned out some of the most respected Bible teachers of their day. Jack Hayford, who is respected far beyond the Pentecostal world, is a recent example.

She was born Aimee Kennedy in Ingersoll, Canada, in 1890. Her father was a Methodist choir director who taught her how to play the piano and organ. If you study her sermons, you will find a wealth of autobiographical information, including references to her early doubts about her faith.

The turning point for Aimee, as I mentioned before, was 1907, the year that John Alexander Dowie died in Zion, Illinois. Aimee Kennedy attended the revival meetings of an itinerant, Pentecostal evangelist named Robert James Semple. Seventeen-year-old Aimee made a commitment to Christ during the revival and fell in love with the evangelist to boot. They were married in the apple orchard of her parents' home.

She was pretty young to be married.

Yes, but early marriage was not all that uncommon at the time, especially in rural communities such as Ingersoll. Aimee's father may have been the local Methodist choir director, but he was also a farmer, and in a farmer's family, the young ladies got married at an early age.

It must have been a remarkable and tantalizing courtship. Robert would have felt some responsibility as Aimee's spiritual mentor. The fact that they literally met at a revival and that they held in common this strong faith in God meant that they must comport themselves with modesty and discretion. At the same time, they felt the natural, normal, physical attraction of a young couple in love. It was a potent mix. To add to the romance, right in the middle of this courtship, Robert and Aimee felt God calling them to be missionaries to China. They would marry and then give their lives to this mysterious, exotic, and faraway land—the most important mission field in the world. It was quite a dream, and it must have been an intoxicating time for the young couple as faith, love, and ambition all stirred together at the same time.

Two years later, after a brief pastorate at a very small church and another few months of a traveling ministry, Robert and Aimee Semple departed for China. The dreams of Ingersoll, Ontario, Canada, were actually coming true.

They arrived in Hong Kong that summer, planning to stay until they had a cursory understanding of one of the popular Chinese languages. Within days, Robert Semple contracted malaria. He died in his young wife's arms. The next month, Aimee Semple gave birth to her first child, Roberta. In September 1910, Aimee Semple, stranded alone in Hong Kong, was a 19-year-old widow with a newborn baby. The dream was over.

There seems to be a lot of pain in all these stories. There is Maria Woodworth-Etter's losing her children, for example.

Well, that's true, but it's also true in the stories of all great people, whether they are religious leaders, sports stars, or leaders of nations. Pain can be a great motivator.

Aimee Semple returned to New York City where she worked for the Salvation Army in a rescue mission. It was a life of service. She was quite poor. But she was gifted with a dynamic personality and great ambition in a good sense of the word. Within a year she was remarried to Harold

Stewart McPherson, a young man her same age. And so the famous compound name of Aimee Semple McPherson was born.

Yet Aimee Semple McPherson didn't have to keep her dead husband's name. She didn't have the same public relations reason of a Maria Woodworth-Etter, who had an established ministry under her previous name. At this time, no one had yet heard of Aimee Semple.

From what I've read, it wasn't all that easy for Aimee to let go of Robert Semple and the dreams they had shared together. It was a natural thing for her to glorify his memory.

Was Harold McPherson a minister?

No, he wasn't. But he was very sympathetic to the call on Aimee's life, at least early in the marriage. In 1913, Aimee gave birth to her second child, Rolf McPherson. But living the life of a traditional mother didn't last long. Eventually, she returned to Canada and held crusades, which some have suspected was her way of retracing Robert Semple's steps and working through part of her grieving process. For a while, Harold McPherson teamed up with her, serving as an advance man and running the business end of the team. It didn't last. Eventually, he returned to the East Coast. They were separated for a number of years, finally divorcing in 1921.

The number of divorces in these stories is staggering. I remember reading about Kathryn Kuhlman's divorce, for example. Was it hard for a man to be married to a celebrity wife or to be married to a wife who was the spiritual authority in the home?

That could be the case. It's true that Maria Woodworth-Etter, Aimee Semple McPherson, and Kathryn Kuhlman were all divorced. It is probably hard for the male ego to be married to someone receiving so much attention on the platform and so much public acclaim. Just as it is supposedly hard for couples in the entertainment industry, when the woman is a super achiever. But then that doesn't explain the divorces among the men. A.A. Allen, for example, was divorced. There was also Clifton Erickson, Richard Roberts, and even myself.

Is it related to the pressures of the ministry?

Well, wait a minute. Before you get carried away, stop and think. Why are these divorces so shocking? The answer is because we don't expect it to happen to a minister. We think somehow that they aren't human. They are different. They should be better. So when something like this does happen to someone in the ministry, it is striking and memorable. This gives us the impression that they are even more prone to divorce than a lay couple or that all ministers are hypocrites. Statistics show just the opposite. While in this country, the average marriage has a 50 percent chance of failure, not even 10 percent of the great healing evangelists experienced a divorce. If one were statistically honest, one would have to say that on a whole their marriages were healthier than the norm, in spite of the perception. The exception to that rule would be the women evangelists, who, admittedly, had a high rate of divorce.

Did the divorce put Aimee Semple McPherson's ministry at risk?

Aimee was briefly ordained in the Assemblies of God denomination, and there are some who suggest she withdrew because of the impending divorce, but a more recent study in the Assemblies of God archives debunks even that theory. From all indications, she weathered the storm pretty handily.

Was there a big break, a Hartford City? Was there one special revival that brought McPherson national acclaim?

The "break," if you want to call it that, was her idea of launching a publication. It was called *The Bridal Call*, which was a reference to the scriptural metaphor of Christ as the groom and the Church as His bride. By today's standards, it was not much of a publication, but it was eagerly read in Pentecostal circles and began to give her a national following. Perhaps more importantly, it helped McPherson begin to discover the power of writing. She wrote a series of books that popularized her teachings and gave her a new respectability.

By the 1920's, Aimee Semple McPherson was speaking in auditoriums and civic centers across the country, sometimes arranging tent crusades, which were still the rage at that time. There was even a much-publicized tour of Australia.

It was in 1921 that the famous 5,000-seat Angelus Temple was built. Aimee always had trouble finding the right place for meetings in southern California. She often used the Shriner's Auditorium, which Kathryn Kuhlman would later use, but there were also times when it wasn't available. The solution lay in building her own place. Thus was born Aimee's church and eventually the denomination called the International Church of the Foursquare Gospel.

What is the Foursquare Gospel?

It's not easy to explain in a sentence or two, but basically it's Aimee Semple McPherson's teaching of "Jesus Christ as Savior, Baptizer, Healer, and Coming King." Foursquare churches were started all over the country, a number of them pastored by women.

We haven't talked about any dramatic healings, and yet Mrs. McPherson is one of the most prominent pioneers in this revival.

Actually, there were thousands of testimonies. People who wrote about the meetings at Angelus Temple describe hundreds of people on stretchers and in wheelchairs being brought in. One of the older members of my own team talks about attending Angelus Temple as a child and hearing the family talk about the healing of his uncle. According to that story, the uncle was in the Veterans Hospital in Van Nuys with cavities in his lungs the size of silver dollars. The family took him up to a service at Angelus Temple. Sister Aimee prayed, and he was healed. Now, that story isn't really documented, but I offer it just to illustrate that there were, in fact, many testimonies and reports of healing that accompanied her meetings.

It is true that, compared to other healing evangelists, there was not the same degree of mysticism surrounding Aimee Semple McPherson's meetings. Part of this may have had something to do with her personality. She was a great showman, and I mean that respectfully. She produced illustrated sermons that became major events in southern California. This was before television, remember. "Sister," as they called her, would recreate Heaven or hell, right on her stage at Angelus Temple. One night she arrived by riding down the center aisle on a motorcycle. Another time she was brought into the church in a coffin. After a long pause, she opened the lid, stood up, and announced her text: "The dead in Christ shall rise first. And then we which remain shall be caught up together with Him in the clouds; and so shall we ever be with the Lord" (see 1 Thess. 4:16-17). The technical crowd from the Hollywood film community was always stopping by to see what she was up to.

Was this a disappointment to the organized Church? I mean, even today we hear criticism about worldly influences in

Christian music or culture. Were there charges that she was cheapening the gospel, that sort of thing?

Of course there was the type of criticism that one would expect to come from jealous pastors who couldn't fill their own small churches. Yet, surprisingly, she had a fair amount of respect from some of the evangelical denominations, including the other Pentecostal groups, which were the most critical of other healing evangelists.

Part of this was because McPherson was a great soul winner. Even the Baptists, who were horrified by the doctrine of healing, had great respect for her. Actually, for a brief period, she held ordination papers with a large Baptist church in California. At that point, Aimee had power within the evangelical world. Her publications had a wide readership, and she was the first evangelist to launch a successful radio broadcast. In fact, she was the first evangelist to obtain an FCC license for a Christian radio station, one that still broadcasts to this day in southern California.

At the same time, the general public saw her as a great relief worker. Taking lessons from her experience with the Salvation Army soup kitchens in New York, Aimee began serving food to the indigent in southern California. There were a number of national stories about it.

Yet before it was all over, McPherson also became extremely controversial.

Oh, she was controversial. From the very beginning, she was controversial. The point I was making was that she was liked. Even while she was controversial, she was respected for what she was doing. Some evangelists were charged with fraud, arrested, or shunned for false doctrine. McPherson escaped that.

Well, I was referring to her alleged kidnapping or disappearance.

That was a major news story, and yes, it would qualify as a scandal. Public opinion shifted after that. Today, Gallup and other pollsters routinely measure the popularity of our religious leaders such as Robert Schuller and Jerry Falwell, but there were no Gallup polls at the time. If there had been, she might have been in trouble. From then on, there were doubts about her. But in terms of her actual ministry, that crisis only increased the crowds.

What happened?

She disappeared. The story was that she had drowned off of Venice Beach. There was even a funeral service for her. It was a national story. Then she showed up in Mexico, claiming to be kidnapped. Well, the international press had a field day. There were charges that she was only having an affair. McPherson stoutly denied it.

Some of the local city fathers were enraged. They had been embarrassed and perhaps a bit jealous of her prominence for years. So they went after her. A grand jury was called, and she was ordered to testify. Later, an aggressive district attorney developed a vendetta against her and pursued her on perjury charges. Eventually, everything was dropped. There just wasn't any evidence. And in a twist reminiscent of John Dowie's fight with the Chicago publisher, the district attorney was soon in trouble with the law himself.

Well, it's still a mystery. There are authors and researchers who lean one way and others who lean the other.

What do you think?

I think she was probably telling the truth, that she really was kidnapped. One of the charges was that she was too cooperative with her kidnappers. But today, after all the analysis surrounding the Patty Hearst kidnapping, we are more knowledgeable about the relationship between kidnappers and their victim. In light of what we know today, I believe she was truthful.

In a way, it's irrelevant. She was human. She did make mistakes. Later on, she experienced one more marriage and a divorce. The secular world never has understood the Christian concept of "grace." They are intimidated by people who believe in absolutes and who are trying to live by a standard. They seize on any failure as evidence that we are hypocritical. They don't seem to hear our claim that we are only sinners, but we are sinners who have thrown ourselves upon the mercy of God and have experienced His forgiveness.

If you are right and she was innocent, then it must have been a bitter experience.

It would have been a bitter experience either way. There is no doubt that she was lonely. She must have continually asked God, "Why?" Why had Robert Semple died, leaving her destitute in China? Why had her marriage failed with Harold McPherson? Why was there the problem that she experienced in her third marriage? Why couldn't she find companionship? Why the loneliness?

In 1930, she had a nervous breakdown, but she recovered. A few years later, her persistent programs for the poor brought her ministry to the verge of bankruptcy, but she recovered from that as well.

Aimee Semple McPherson died in 1944. She was found in her hotel room. She had apparently, accidentally, taken an overdose of a prescribed medicine. Ironically, almost 25 years later, A.A. Allen would die in a hotel room only a few miles away under similar circumstances. Her ministry was strong. Her son Rolf had already been named as her successor. The International Church of the Foursquare Gospel and all their highly respected and talented ministers are her legacy.

Which brings us to Kathryn Kuhlman.

Well, unlike Aimee Semple McPherson, Kathryn Kuhlman was definitely mystical. Her ministry is defined by the thousands of documented miracles of healing. *Time* magazine called her a "one woman Shrine of Lourdes."

Kathryn Kuhlman was already a 16-year-old itinerant evangelist, touring the West, when Aimee Semple McPherson was in her prime. She would have read about McPherson's kidnapping in the newspapers.

In 1933, Kathryn Kuhlman settled down in Denver with plans to build her own Angelus Temple, although she would have bristled at any comparison to McPherson; she was much too original for that. By 1935, she was filling the 2,000-seat Kuhlman Revival Tabernacle and had launched a radio program. Even early in her ministry, she was deeply aware of the power of the press and was somehow able to build relationships that always eluded Oral Roberts and the very biggest and best public relations-minded of the great healing evangelists. Perhaps it is overstating things to say she was the toast of Denver, but she had as much favor as a healing evangelist could possibly hope for.

And then there was scandal.

Burroughs A. Waltrip came to town. He was an evangelist, and he was a married man. They fell in love, and Waltrip left his wife to marry Kathryn Kuhlman. They thought that they could weather the storm. But her ministry in Denver was destroyed. Six years later, that marriage broke up as well, and Kathryn Kuhlman returned to a traveling evangelistic ministry.

It was not an easy road. She would have a great crusade with wonderful results, and then word would come to town about her marriage and divorce. There would be the charges that she was a "home wrecker," and she would be forced to move onto the next town. No denomination worked with her. It was a lonely time.

When the full tide of the healing revival hit the nation in the 1950's, Kathryn Kuhlman's ministry lay dormant. She stayed put in Pennsylvania and Ohio, where there were beautiful services with many marvelous miracles, yet she was not nationally known. Perhaps, because she had been hurt so badly in the past, she did nothing to promote herself. But her low-key approach contrasted with the flamboyance of the other evangelists, and it won her quiet support among a small, select group, including Presbyterians, Methodists, and other traditional Christians, even Roman Catholics. In the 1960's and 70's, when the charismatic renewal would hit, her ministry would seemingly come out of nowhere and sweep the nation.

Actually, the ministry of Kathryn Kuhlman was a lifetime in the making. In its own way, it was born with just as much pain as the births of the ministries of Maria Woodworth-Etter and Aimee Semple McPherson. But God had not abandoned Kathryn Kuhlman during her time of exile in the 1940's and 50's. He was just refining her for something even better. Before it was all over, she would reemerge as one of the greatest of the healing evangelists of this century.

Chapter Three

A National Phenomenon— the Healing Revival

Charles Price, Earl Ivy, and William Branham

In the late 1940's, the full force of the healing revival broke across North America and the world. There were literally thousands of evangelists with a revival tent almost on every corner. Huge auditoriums were built, and the Pentecostal denominations began a remarkable growth cycle that has continued to this day, especially in Latin America.

The last of the forerunners of this really massive movement was an Oxford-trained, Canadian Methodist named Charles Price. His great ministry took place just before the floodgates opened and the movement reached its peak.

Charles Price was a brilliant orator and thinker. During World War I he gained some notoriety as a professional speaker selling American war bonds to theater audiences in San Francisco. Early on, he was for all intents and purposes a "modernist" minister, even questioning the Virgin Birth. Of course, this got him in trouble with his Methodist bishop, and eventually, Price changed denominations, taking over a pastorate in the Congregationalist Church, a denomination in which the local members had sovereignty, not an Episcopal hierarchy. In 1920, he visited an Aimee Semple McPherson crusade in San Jose, California. He later said that he had gone more out of curiosity than for any other reason, although the fact that members of his own congregation were attending was probably irksome and may have helped prompt him to check it out. Price was mentally prepared to take apart the simplistic message he expected to hear. Instead, "Sister Aimee" preached what Price later called a "masterful message," exposing the emptiness and absurdity of the modernist doctrines. Price was shaken. He returned each night thereafter, eventually responding to the altar call.

Two years later, Charles Price was conducting crusades all across Canada and the Northwest. In Victoria, a local journalist wrote a story that included reports of several remarkable healings, and then the circus really began. Crowds filled auditoriums an hour before the services were supposed to begin. Sometimes they broke the windows to get in. Sometimes the fire marshall would shut the meeting down because of the crowds. At other times the meeting would become delayed because Price himself couldn't get into the auditorium to deliver his sermon. In some cities, churches got together and began building auditoriums to host crusades.

Again, it's hard to understand how the crowds come so suddenly. It seems to be the same phenomenon with each story: A minister will work hard for years and see no growth, but some of these evangelists seem to have huge audiences instantly. There is a dynamic that is missing here.

And once again, I have to say that the "phenomenon" occurs because something is happening. The most eloquent and entertaining speaker with the most organized staff and facility cannot attract the numbers that will come if people really believe that something is going to happen and that there is a chance for a miracle in their life. Doctrine is wonderful, but reality is even better.

I guess I should add that what drew a lot of curiosity and criticism to the Charles Price meetings were the so-called experiences of "falling under the power" or being "slain in the Spirit." Often when Price would pray for someone, they would fall over on the floor in a trance. Then it started happening all the time. Sometimes it would sweep across the audience like a wave, and thousands would fall over.

Did this phenomenon begin with Charles Price?

No, it has a lineage as old as healing itself. Remember when they came for Jesus in the Garden of Gethsemane, and He said, "I am He."

The Bible says they fell over as if knocked to the ground (see Jn. 18:6). I haven't really researched it throughout Church history, but I would be very surprised if it didn't occasionally surface in various healing or miracle ministries. It happened in Smith Wigglesworth's time, and yet *it was not the dominant characteristic of a Wigglesworth meeting*. One gets the feeling that this phenomenon was not always present in his services.

Yet, one could say that in recent history, Charles Price is more commonly associated with the phenomenon of being "slain in the Spirit" and that his ministry helped to popularize it.

What is it? Is it a genuine manifestation, or is it simply psychological?

It's real. It happens in my ministry today, which is mostly a ministry in Third World countries. I will often pray for people who know absolutely nothing about it and have never even heard about it, and they will suddenly feel God's power and go limp and fall over. It happens today in Benny Hinn's crusades.

So to answer your question, yes. It's real, but it can also be psychological. People who want to experience the power of God and want to fall will fall. There are also people who don't want to fall and who are steeled against it, and these will work themselves up into such a state of mind that, by the time they get near the evangelist, they will often fall too. Sometimes when a person doesn't care one way or the other, he or she won't fall.

The exception to that was when Kathryn Kuhlman, Bill Branham, or Charles Price were in their prime. No one stood a chance then. The most hardened skeptic would just drop like a leaf. It had to be more than psychological. Sometimes the person being slain in the Spirit had his or her back to the evangelist and didn't even know he or she was coming by, but that person would fall over anyway.

I have to tell you an amusing story. One of the major television networks recently targeted a healing ministry. This ministry was not known for people being "slain in the Spirit," but it did occasionally happen. Well, when the story aired on television, it was a monstrosity. Allegedly the network had spliced words into the interviews to change the meaning. They had allegedly planted their own "evidence" and then reported on it. Naturally, the ministry sued. But in the process, all the network's raw video footage had to be given to the ministry.

Well, it turns out that, unbeknownst to the ministry, the television network had planted one of their undercover women reporters in the service. Naturally, she was all wired for sound and with a hidden camera. Well, at the end of the service this hostile reporter went forward for prayer, just to see what would happen. When the minister touched her, she fell over. The video shows the ceiling, the audio picks up her voice, cursing and mumbling into the microphone, "Wow, what was that? I think I see why these people fall over."

So, to answer your questions, yes it is spiritual, and yes it is probably psychological. In the ministry of Charles Price, it helped attract huge crowds, and people really believed that they were experiencing the power of God. There was great faith and a holy awe. People would repent, confess their sins, and get right with God.

But in itself, what value does it have?

The Bible teaches that God is a Spirit, but we humans are very much physical as well as spiritual beings. This phenomenon is something you can see and feel. It's physical. Jesus says that things of the Spirit are like the wind. You can't see it. You don't know where it comes from or where it is going, but you know that it has been there. When this phenomenon sweeps through, it is like the wind. You see the human, physical reaction to an encounter with the Holy Spirit. It frightens some people. Sometimes it shocks them into the reality of the spiritual world and forces them to confront their spiritual situation. For some people, it may not come across very well on television. Perhaps that is what Jesus warned about when He said not to reveal spiritual things to those who weren't ready. He called it giving pearls to swine (see Mt. 7:6). But to those very skeptical, critical people who walked into a Charles Price crusade with the intention of mentally exposing the fraud and found themselves knocked flat on their fanny when he pointed a finger in their direction, well, it was kind of a miracle. And it was the stuff of legend.

But there were healings too?

There were marvelous healings. In 1923, Lorne Fox, a young concert pianist and student, was healed of a serious heart condition in a Charles Price crusade. Fox became an evangelist himself, and curiously, the phenomenon of being slain in the Spirit started happening in his meetings as well. Out of the Fox crusades came a young, converted artist named Willard Cantelon who became the great missionary-evangelist. You can see the link down through the generations.

In the tradition of the other great evangelists, Charles Price soon began to take his message to the world. He traveled across Europe and the Middle East, with a series of remarkable crusades in Islamic Turkey. Lorne Fox and his team traveled even more extensively worldwide. And finally, Willard Cantelon became something of an international Christian statesman, living for many years in Geneva.

When did the proliferation of healing evangelists really start?

It started in the late 1940's, right at the tail end of the Charles Price ministry. Some, such as Lorne Fox, were directly inspired by Price. Others were inspired by the writings and stories of Aimee Semple McPherson, Smith Wigglesworth, and the Pentecostal denominational pioneers of divine healing such as Charles Parham who had links back to John Dowie. Remember Kathryn Kuhlman was still going at this time, although until the 1960's she stayed pretty much to herself and had only a limited, devoted following.

Some cite Franklin Hall as one of the men who helped spark the revival. He was a poor, uneducated, independent preacher. In 1946, he wrote a small booklet with the unlikely title of *Atomic Power Through Prayer and Fasting*. Considering that it was only privately published, it had an amazing impact. Some criticized Hall as an extremist, and he did have some rather radical ideas, but many of the early healing evangelists of the late 1940's learned from Hall.

Another one was Earl Ivy. He was a Jewish convert who had been raised in an orphanage. At one time, he owned huge tracts of land in what is now Anaheim. Anyway, Ivy bought a giant tent from Army surplus. It could seat thousands. He had a healing ministry, but he was also a renowned soul winner. He built a small pool right on his property that he called the Pool of Bethesda. Allegedly as many as 4,000 people were baptized there on a single night.

One visitor was Dr. Thomas Wyatt from Portland, Oregon. His wife was apparently dying when Ivy prayed for her. Well, as the story goes, she was healed. Ivy supposedly gave Wyatt $1,000 and told him to go back to Portland where God would give him a worldwide ministry. Wyatt went back, launched a radio program, and wound up on the old Mutual Broadcasting System, which at the time broadcast worldwide. There were hundreds of others like Franklin Hall and Earl Ivy. But by far, most of the new healing evangelists of the late 1940's were inspired by a poor, humble, backroads preacher named William Branham. And when I say poor, I mean "dirt poor." Branham was born in a log cabin with dirt floors. There was no running water. And we're talking about the twentieth century!

In his early years, Branham had very limited gifts as a public speaker. But he was an extraordinary mystic. He had faith to believe that things would happen. And, as a result, they usually did. In the 1930's he built what they later called the Branham Tabernacle in Jeffersonville, Indiana.

Where did he come from? What was his denominational background?

He was born in Kentucky, but the family moved to Indiana not long after his birth. To answer your question, he really came out of nowhere. No one even recorded the exact date of his birth.

His father was only 18 years old. His mother was only 15. Get ready, this is quite a story. After the midwife delivered the Branham baby, she laid him on his mother's stomach and went over to open the window. Actually, there was no glass, just a wooden shutter. Well, according to the story, the sunshine poured into the room along with a little light about one foot in diameter, the size of a halo. Anyway, this little light floated in and settled over the baby's head.

Neither one of the Branhams were religious, but the incident at his birth so astounded them that they took him to the nearest church to ask the pastor about it. It happened to be a Baptist church. Later, in Indiana, young Bill Branham became a regular member of a Baptist congregation. His youth was one of incredible hardship. The boy had an old hand-me-down coat that was held together with safety pins. For a long time, he wore it everywhere and never even took it off in school for the simple reason that he didn't own a shirt. So his background was one of abject poverty.

His story seems to fit the formula. It seems to be the same story for so many of these men and women.

Branham's father was an alcoholic, which will also fit the formula of so many evangelists to follow. Sometimes his father would just disappear for several months at a time. Several times young Bill Branham and his mother almost starved to death.

As a youth, he had flashes of the mysticism that would later make him famous. Branham claimed that he heard a voice from strong wind blowing through some trees. The voice told him to "stay away from strong drink, or tobacco, or anything that will defile your body. When you are older, I have a work for you to do."

Was this a conversion experience?

Oh, no. It was nothing like that. His conversion came much later. He even had several visions as a youth. One day he was playing along the Ohio river when he suddenly saw a huge bridge growing out of the Kentucky side toward Indiana. As the bridge moved toward him, he counted 16 men falling to their deaths. The vision so troubled him that he told everybody who would listen. Years later, when the Municipal Bridge was built, and one by one men accidentally fell to their deaths until there were exactly 16, his family was astounded. Barnham had described it all as a boy.

Later, when he began his healing ministry, he quickly had a devoted, local following. They had known for years that there was something special about him.

What happened? How did he convert?

Well, you've heard this before, and you might as well get used to it because you will hear it again. As a young adult, he became deathly ill. Out of desperation, he sought God to spare his life. In the process he had a number of mystical experiences that would likely have been dismissed as the ramblings of an overactive imagination if it had not been for what would happen later. For example, one day, during a time of prayer, a bright light entered the room. Young Branham panicked and ran outside, but after calming down, he said, "If that's really You, Lord, let the light come back." He went back inside, and the light reappeared. Of course, Branham claimed a healing. His doctor was astounded. Soon afterward, the young man felt God calling him to preach and pray for the sick. It was the same old story.

And there were huge crowds?

Well, yes and no. This guy's story is a little bit different. At first, he started working with a local pastor of the Baptist church. And yes, there was a huge tent revival with some amazing miracles. The Baptist pastor didn't really know how to react. His denomination didn't believe in that sort of thing, but Branham was his own young convert and was very submissive and humble. The miracles were undeniable. There wasn't much he could do about it. Almost 3,000 people came to this first revival.

What sort of thing happened? Are you talking about healing?

As I understand it, his great healing ministry hadn't quite gotten started yet. In the Baptist tradition, his emphasis was on salvation and baptism. But, for example, as he began baptizing people, a strange light appeared over his head. Thousands of people saw it and pointed at it. There was a big commotion over it. Even the local newspaper ran a story about it. Well, the pastor could hardly deny what he had seen. He could dismiss its significance but he couldn't deny that it had happened. Eventually, over time, the converts from this very first revival organized themselves and built what came to be called the Branham Tabernacle. So it was a pretty impressive start.

One would think that Baptists would have been more skeptical and even critical of such mysticism.

Well, he was a boy. And people who were a part of those beginnings say that his testimony was so tender, humble, and sincere that it just totally disarmed his listeners.

You say that the new converts from this meeting organized themselves. Wasn't Branham their leader? Where was he during all this?

He wasn't quite ready to assume any great leadership role. He spoke at a few Baptist churches, but not much happened. Like his father and mother, Bill Branham ended up getting married fairly young. He and his wife, Hope Brumback, had a little daughter. They wanted to take a name from the Bible and couldn't decide. They liked the expressive reference to the Messiah as the *Rose of Sharon*, so they ended up naming her Sharon Rose. When a little boy came along they named him Billy Paul. Branham continued to preach wherever he could get an invitation, but that didn't bring in enough money to support them so he eventually hired on as an Indiana game warden.

Then he experienced a great crisis of the soul. One day he passed by an open-air Pentecostal revival meeting. The singing was enthusiastic and the mood contagious. Well, there were a lot of ministers present and each one, including Branham, were introduced. Branham returned each night and was eventually invited up to give his testimony. Evidently, his sincerity and tenderness struck a chord with the Pentecostals, and he was bombarded with invitations to speak at churches across the country.

When Branham told his Baptist pastor friend about his experience and the invitations, he was met with a stern rebuke. He was told that these people were "trashy" and that his association with them would ruin his reputation. Not only were these people Pentecostals, but they were Oneness; that is, they believed that new converts should be baptized in the name of Jesus only, not the Father, the Son, and Holy Ghost. Against his better judgment, Branham declined the invitations. Then disaster struck. His father died of a heart attack at the young age of 52. Then his brother died, and his wife contracted a serious lung infection.

In 1937, a dike broke near Jeffersonville, Indiana, and the little city was practically wiped off the map. Since Branham was an Indiana game warden, he was recruited into action. For days he raced all over the county rescuing people from their homes. And then he learned that a second dike had broken and that his own neighborhood had been flooded. Everyone who had survived, including, he hoped, his wife and children, were on a cattle car, being evacuated to a nearby town. Branham raced across the state, trying to find them, while at the same time attending to dozens of life-and-death emergencies along the way.

After a week, he was in a state of near panic, when a local volunteer told him that the train car he had been looking for had been washed off the tracks. There had been many injuries and most of the people had disappeared into the water. Branham threw himself on the ground, calling out to God to save his family, promising to be obedient to whatever God wanted for his life. He raced from town to town searching for his family. Finally, after several days, he found a railroad official who remembered a young mother with two children. They were very sick, he was warned. The official also remembered that the baby had not looked like she was going to make it.

Bill Branham finally caught up with his family in a makeshift hospital in the Baptist church in Columbus, Indiana. His wife, Hope, had lost almost 30 pounds. She was a skeleton, and the doctor said she was dying of a very advanced form of tuberculosis. There was nothing that anyone could do. The children were at another center, in isolation. The doctors were hopeful that the mother hadn't passed on the deadly disease.

Branham wept and rocked his wife in his arms, crying out to God to spare her. The nurses couldn't stand it. They left them alone. And finally, mercifully, Hope died in her husband's arms. Within days, it became apparent that Sharon Rose was dying as well. Young Branham was finally, forcefully, prevented from seeing the little girl. They were afraid that he would carry germs to the other child, young Billy Paul. It was torture for the young father. He could hear the baby scream out for her mother, not knowing or understanding that she was gone. Finally, Branham pushed his way into the back of the building and found his daughter in an isolation ward in the basement. He took Sharon Rose in his arms and held her hour after hour until she too died.

His son, Billy Paul, survived, but Branham forever blamed himself for the death of his wife and daughter, saying that he had been disobedient in rejecting God's call to preach. He believed that it all started with his refusal to speak to the Pentecostal Apostolics, or so-called "Jesus only" churches. That was the door God had opened for him, humble as it may have been, and he had refused to go in.

That's pretty severe.

Yes, this isn't Robert Schuller. This is pretty tough stuff. Franklin Hall and many of the other divine healing pioneers were just as fanatical. Although, interesting enough, the so-called prosperity gospel was eventually born out of the healing revival. But that comes later.

The same formula is repeating itself. Does God require pain to give birth to this type of ministry?

I don't see how one could build a whole theology on that notion from the Scriptures. But it is very clear that pain has a refining influence on the soul, and God is not above using it, after the fact, to bring something good from it. Remember the words of Joseph when he confronted his brothers who had sold him into slavery? "You meant it for evil, but God meant it for good" (see Gen. 50:20).

We have transcripts from some of Branham's meetings, and in one of them he describes his last moments with Sharon Rose. He said that she was in such pain that she was having stomach spasms and was using all of her energy just to manage the pain. She knew he was there, but didn't have the strength to smile or speak. He said that the pain was so great that when she looked at him her eyes crossed. Branham said that when he looked into the face of a child with crossed eyes, he saw his little girl, and it gave him compassion to believe in that child's healing. At the time, more than 400 children with crossed eyes had been healed in his meetings. Branham's comment was that sometimes God had to crush a rose to bring forth its fragrance.

When there is pain, some people react just the opposite. It can be used as an occasion to reject the idea of a personal God.

Well, now the story gets pretty mystical, so hold on. Once more there is the coincidence of everything happening in the same year. Those of us evangelicals who believe in the supernatural would say that it is no coincidence at all; we would believe that some divine destiny was at work. However, in 1946, a miracle occurred in the middle of a Kathryn Kuhlman service. A woman was healed of a tumor. It was a very clear-cut healing that thousands of people could see with their own eyes. It was a turning point for the Kuhlman ministry. From then on, she began to call out healing right in the middle of her services. "Someone in the balcony is being healed of cancer. Over there—yes, you, the lady in the red dress."

While this, rather sensational, manifestation of the Spirit began to take place in the limited world of the Kathryn Kuhlman meetings, that same year, on May 7, 1946, William Branham had what he claimed was a visit from an angel. Branham said that the angel announced that he had come directly from the presence of God and that he, Bill Branham, was going to be given a special gift to pray for the sick. He was told that he would soon be speaking before thousands of people, taking to them God's message of healing. Almost immediately, the crowds began coming.

Here we go again?

Well, this was different. Yes, there were outstanding healings and that was primarily why the crowds came. And yes, there was often the phenomenon of "falling under the power," but it was much more dramatic than in other comparable settings of the day. Sometimes when Branham would pray for the sick, he would first tell the person all about themselves—where they were from, what they were praying about, sometimes revealing secrets that no one but the person could possibly know. The reaction was predictable. It was like a scene out of the Bible from when the Old Testament prophets had that power or when Jesus could read people's thoughts. A wave of conviction would sweep over his audiences. People wept and repented. And then, it started happening regularly, night after night, person after person. Often, Branham would take the person aside and privately tell them about sins in their life.

What was it all about?

Today, theologians would call it the word of knowledge, which is one of the nine gifts of the Spirit, or *charismata* of the New Testament

Church. Back then, the Pentecostals had barely gotten healing and speaking in tongues under their belt.

But it was real?

Oh, it was real. This was not some parlor trick. There were no hidden microphones or hand signals. Eventually, journalists from all over the world covered the meetings. The sick were lined up by the thousands. Many people were taken to meetings right from the hospitals on stretchers. A journalist would have loved to expose anything fraudulent.

Later on, when Branham began to travel the world, the same gift worked in other countries, where he had no knowledge or understanding of the language. Ministers often brought him sick people from their own congregations, people whom they personally knew and whose integrity they could vouch for. It didn't matter who was brought to him; even at random, he could sometimes even call them by their name and they were people who had never seen him before. One pastor friend of mine took a relative to him, and Branham described in minute detail things about his life, including things that he had thought. The pastor's relative began weeping, saying, "It's true." In such an atmosphere, the people's faith was great and astounding miracles began to occur.

The great Pentecostal leader F.F. Bosworth, who sat under John Dowie as a child and served as the host pastor to a crusade held by Maria Woodworth-Etter, described the Branham meetings as far more powerful than the other two. No disease or problem seemed too big. Bosworth told of one meeting where nine deaf mutes appeared in a healing line, and all nine of them were healed.

Then Branham began to tell audiences about visions he was receiving. He would describe a bedroom with a sick child. He would describe the wallpaper design and things that were hung on the wall, the pattern of the bedspread, a description of a scene with the local doctor and a recounting of an exact conversation. Well, letters would come in from parents all over the world, saying that maybe this was their child's bedroom and their child. Eventually, the right one would arrive, even with an exact recounting of the conversation with the local doctor. Bill Branham would publicly announce it and then go to the child. He would pray, and there would be a healing.

This happened on several occasions. He would publicly announce a miracle before it would happen, invoking many small details, pushing it away beyond the possibility of chance. When it finally occurred, there was great amazement. So maybe you can understand why there were crowds overnight. They came from everywhere. At first the meetings were held in small, rural, country towns. But the people would find him anyway. As in the case of Charles Price before him, the auditoriums were packed hours before he arrived. Sometimes people camped all night on the steps.

The stories of healing crossed every ethnic and religious barrier. And Branham was so obviously uneducated and humble that people believed him when he gave all the credit to God. There was no denominational awareness in his crusades. People were united as one, and they were all full of awe as they waited for what God would do. Branham spoke in hushed, quiet tones, which was a deep contrast to the bombastic evangelists who would succeed him. There was a deep, deep sense of faith and of fear as well. There was this group awareness: It's real. There is a God. He does love us, and the warnings He gives us through the prophets are true also. It's true.

In Fort Wayne, Indiana, an evangelical college that was very much against the doctrine of divine healing forbade their students from attending the meetings. But for some reason, they made one exception. Secretly, they allowed one young blind girl and her instructor to go and check it out.

Well, by this time, Branham, feeling inadequate as a preacher, had brought a gifted speaker, Ern Baxter, onto his team. Baxter would deliver the sermons each night, and then Branham would come out at the end and pray for the sick. Sure enough, as soon as Branham started praying for the sick, he stopped, turned to the middle of the audience, and pointed his finger. "There's a young lady out there who is being healed of blindness. She is a student, and she is here with one of her teachers."

The girl let out a scream and jumped to her feet crying and praising God. There was pandemonium. Finally, they calmed everybody down, and the shocked teacher listened as the young blind girl started describing the things she could see around the room. The college officials were shaken. But we must give them credit. They didn't know what else to do, so they closed the school and ordered the students to the Branham crusade.

One would think that if the healings were documented that there would be more acceptance of them. I mean, either a story like that is true or it is not true.

Remember, Jesus told a story about a man who died, and from his place in hell he called out and asked Abraham to warn his brothers back on earth. Abraham replied that God had warned his brothers and that He had sent the prophets. "Well, they won't believe the prophets," the man said. "But if you would only send someone back from the dead, then they would believe." But Abraham said, "No, he wouldn't believe, even if God sent someone back from the dead." (See Luke 16.)

There are some people who just won't believe—in fact, most people. Jesus said that spiritual things are spiritually discerned. And that must surely include healing.

But when a healing takes place, how does the unbeliever rationalize what has happened?

Well, you know how one rationalizes? The skeptics say it's "suggestion" or "hysteria." Today, it may also be referred to as "paranormal," meaning, "yes, it exists but it's a special gift that a select few people have and is not related to a supernatural world." Margaret Mead, for one, has helped make paranormal studies one of the legitimate branches of science. Today science is trying to co-opt divine healing, but what about in Bill Branham's time, in the late 1940's and 50's? The skeptics and, in fact, the leaders in society simply denied that it was taking place. They would just say, "No, that did not happen."

But what about the girl who was blind and her family, they couldn't deny it?

People who were directly affected by a miracle usually were convinced, but even then, sometimes, they rationalized—"My sight was coming back anyway and this event just provided the shock." Sure, there was denial.

Remember too that William Branham was not an educated man. There were no great apologists among the Pentecostals, who basically sprung up from a poor white and black American culture. They were socially despised, and at the same time, they felt no need to defend what was happening. There was no great effort to document these healings. Why should there be? Those who believed in healing didn't need it. They were seeing with their own eyes and experiencing for themselves.

I remember attending several Branham crusades as a young child. The excitement and anticipation was almost palpable. There was almost a sense of panic about whether one would get a seat. You couldn't get up, even to go to the men's room, or your seat would be gone. There were almost as many outside

wanting to get in as there were in the auditorium. I kept wondering why it wasn't on the front pages of the newspapers? The whole city would shut down when he came to town.

In some cases it was on the front pages. In 1951, a California congressman by the name of William Upshaw was healed. He had been crippled since birth. Some of these stories made the wire and captured headlines. When Branham traveled overseas, many heads of state were curious to meet him. The King of England sent a telegram asking for prayer. But you are right that in many respects, Branham's ministry was a phenomenon that spread through the grass roots of America almost undetected by media and social leaders. Individual towns were sometimes greatly impacted. There are civic centers still standing that were essentially built to house a William Branham crusade. But the nation as a whole did not celebrate him.

Part of that had to do with his own humility. He was surprisingly unaffected by all the attention. Sometimes his hosts would put him in the nicest hotel in town and he would check out and find a very cheap motel and stay there instead. He explained that it was too nice for him and that he wasn't that important since God was the one doing all the healing anyway. He encouraged them to use the extra money for the other expenses. This happened frequently.

Branham was famous for wearing very inexpensive J.C. Penney suits. There was a story about him arriving late to one of his own crusades. There were thousands of people crowded outside the doors, unable to get into the auditorium. Branham was moving unnoticed through this crowd when he found a lost little black child. The boy was crying, saying that he was blind and that he and his parents had come for a healing, but that now they weren't going to get in to see the man who prays for the sick and that he was lost.

Branham said, "Well, I'm the man who prays for the sick and Jesus is the man who heals them. You are not lost. You are found. And Jesus is going to heal you now." Branham prayed. The little black boy was healed and started shouting. Suddenly, this frustrated and disappointed crowd realized that it was William Branham in their midst. Some of them had driven for thousands of miles only to be shut outside because there was no room. Well, they rushed him, just trying to touch him for their healing or trying to get a piece of his clothes to take back to their sick loved one. Within seconds, this mob of people had ripped his J.C. Penney's suit to shreds, and police who were on hand for crowd control had to rescue him and get him back to his hotel for another change of clothes.

The Branham phenomenon took place just before television. Had it occurred ten years later, he would be a household name today.

How did the organized Church react?

They were threatened. There was no room for him within traditional Christianity. At the time, the Catholic church did not recognize believers outside their own faith. The Episcopalians, Methodists, and Baptists had already expelled Pentecostals for believing in such things as healing and speaking in tongues. The Fundamentalists, who rejected anything miraculous, openly attacked him, saying that his power was demonic.

And his fellow Pentecostals?

Well, that was complex too. Some Pentecostals were suspicious of his Baptist origins. Then, others were upset by his association with the Apostolics, or "Jesus Only" believers, who promoted the Oneness doctrine. The Assemblies of God, Church of God, and other Pentecostals were basically Trinitarian, or traditional, in their belief that one should be baptized in the name of the Father, the Son, and the Holy Spirit. It was a big debate, and it was hot. The division was great.

The Assemblies of God was by far the biggest denomination, but Bill Branham, remembering the price of his earlier refusal to minister to the Oneness, or Apostolics, sided with them. While many rank and file pastors in the Assemblies of God and Church of God welcomed him to town, others felt threatened. Would they lose their people? The general superintendent of the Assemblies of God, Gayle F. Lewis, received so much mail that he eventually ordered an investigation. The report came back that it was true. The miracles were for real. But to their own discredit, the Assemblies of God chose to officially ignore William Branham, just as years later they would ignore the charismatic renewal in the Catholic church.

At the same time, many of Branham's own Apostolic brothers criticized him for not openly preaching their important Oneness doctrine at his crusades. Branham constantly stressed the unity of all believers, a message that he claimed had been given to him from his 1946 angelic visit. But some critical Apostolics accused him of compromising their important doctrine.

Tell me about the team that he put together. By this time he was an industry.

Well, there was Ern Baxter, the powerful preacher and orator. And there was Jack Moore, a fellow Oneness minister and personal friend. But the most significant addition was a friend of Moore's named Gordon Lindsay. Lindsay was an Assembly of God pastor from Ashland, Oregon, who went on to become one of the most important figures in the healing movement, perhaps *the* most important figure.

Gordon Lindsay encouraged Branham to avoid doctrinal controversies in his crusades and to seek common denominators that would widen his audience and carry the message of healing to other denominations. Branham was ready to hear this since it corresponded to the message that the angelic visitor had brought him, "the unity of all believers."

Lindsay's greatest contribution lay in organizing and promoting Bill Branham's crusades. You really have to give him much of the credit for the effectiveness of Branham's so-called "union meetings," where all the local Pentecostal congregations were united to sponsor a crusade. This was the formula that all the later healing evangelists would follow. Eventually, Lindsay would write several books about Branham. Almost immediately, he launched *The Voice of Healing* magazine, which reported on the meetings and served as a critically important common denominator for the whole healing revival.

And yet the Bill Branham ministry peaked. It eventually ran its course, with Gordon Lindsay going on to help lead and organize for others.

As with all of us, Branham's strengths were his weaknesses too. He was very sincere and humble and very mystical. Sometimes he would only pray for a few people and then would announce that he did not feel "the anointing" and could not continue without it. He would just declare the service over. Sometimes he would pray for 30 people and then collapse, unable to continue. Well, there were tens of thousands of people, some of them very poor, spending their money to travel great distances to be prayed for, and these persons would often feel disappointed or let down if Branham could not pray for them.

Most damaging of all were those times when he would just not come. You couldn't count on him. He would cancel in the last minute, saying that it wasn't God's will or that he "felt a check." You can imagine the consternation. Usually a whole city had worked together to bring him in. Many churches were involved, and there were expenses and advertising invested in the meeting.

Didn't he actually quit for a while?

That was the big crisis. In 1948, he suddenly announced that he was burned out and would have to leave his crusade circuit because, of all things, he was suffering "ill health"! Gordon Lindsay was dumbfounded. He and his colleagues had scheduled Branham in every major city in America. An organization was finally in place. William Branham, notwithstanding the controversy of the healing message, was on the verge of becoming the most celebrated and important national religious figure since Billy Sunday.

The news stunned and confused his devoted followers who didn't know what else to do but to begin praying for his full recovery. Each night, a young, new, popular evangelist by the name of Oral Roberts had his tent congregations pray for Bill Branham.

Within a few months, Branham declared himself fit after all and returned to his ministry. This time, the reputable F.F. Bosworth agreed to serve as a senior advisor to the evangelist. Gordon Lindsay even came back to help out. But in the interim, *The Voice of Healing* magazine had begun featuring other emerging evangelists as well. Gordon Lindsay was not going to put all his eggs into one basket again. This was a decision that would help spark the proliferation of new ministries and trigger the explosion of the healing movement.

There is the theory that Branham needed to prove something as a preacher.

Within time, there was so much curiosity and such a demand for him that audiences wanted to hear him preach even if it was not a dynamic sermon. After all, he was a good man of God, and they wanted to hear from him. What did he think? And as is true with anything, if you do something enough, you begin to get good at it. Thus, Branham began to develop as a preacher, eventually preaching his own services again. His style was tender and self-deprecating. He was so humble, always identifying himself with poor. People loved him for that, and that was one of the major reasons that other healing evangelists harbored little jealousy toward him. By the mid-1950's, Branham had become an especially entertaining and insightful speaker, especially when speaking to his fellow ministers.

The great legacy of the William Branham ministry can be seen in the hundreds and thousands of other similar ministries that he inspired.

To many observers and historians, Branham was the father of the great healing revival of the mid-twentieth century. His humility and willingness to give all the credit to God, provoked a boldness and a courageousness among many others who believed that they too could be used of God. His union meetings became the prototype. By 1950, when Gordon Lindsay called for a national *Voice of Healing* convention, more than 1,000 new healing evangelists came. The great healing revival of the mid-twentieth century was on.

Chapter Four

"God Is a Good God!"

T.L. Osborn, Oral Roberts,
Morris Cerullo, and Jack Coe

Now try to get the sense of timing in all of this. In 1946 William Branham was visited by an angel who told him that he was to take a message of healing to the world. That same year, a remarkable healing takes place in a Kathryn Kuhlman crusade in Pennsylvania. From then on, her ministry became even more dynamic; she began to point out people in her audience who had been healed.

Meanwhile, still in 1946, a poor, itinerant Methodist evangelist by the name of Franklin Hall privately published a book with the unlikely title of *Atomic Power Through Prayer and Fasting*. Hall was considered eccentric by other evangelists who would follow him. He was never to have a truly great ministry, but his book that was written in 1946 was to have an uncanny influence on all who would follow.

That same year, William Freeman, a poor Pentecostal pastor in Salem, Oregon, lay dying of cancer. His wife became overwhelmed and suffered a nervous breakdown. Perhaps influenced by Hall, Freeman began fasting and praying, night after night, pleading for a miracle. Finally, one night he had a vision. Freeman claimed to have seen Jesus standing on a cloud with this scene slowly dissolving into another that showed Freeman speaking before a vast audience, praising God for his miracle. Within days the cancer began to remit. By the end of the year he was completely healed.

Meanwhile, thousands of miles away in India, a missionary from Oklahoma named T.L. Osborn contracted typhoid fever. His baby was dangerously ill of cholera. He and his wife were almost ready to give up their ministry. Within months, they were on their way back to the United States, viewing their mission to India as a failure.

In 1946, a World War II veteran and alcoholic named David Oliver Nunn was converted. He too rose to be a leader in the great healing movement.

And, finally, that same year—in 1946—while William Freeman experienced his healing from cancer and the Osborns were on their way back to the United States, another young minister in Oklahoma by the name of Oral Roberts was feeling discouraged and defeated in his ministry and began a seven-month period of special prayer and fasting.

These were the birth pains of the great deluge that were about to hit. Then came 1947. Within a period of a few days, Smith Wigglesworth and Charles Price both died. But that same year, the full force of the healing movement broke across the United States and, eventually, the world. Believe me, it was something to behold.

In 1947, William Freeman, the poor Pentecostal preacher who was healed of cancer, began holding crusades in California. Gordon Lindsay traveled out to see what was going on and was amazed. *The Voice of Healing* began regular reports on Freeman's ministry, and huge crowds came out to see him.

In 1947, T.L. Osborn, the missionary from India, visited a William Branham meeting in Oregon. Branham was praying for a little deaf girl and was quietly but forcefully commanding the spirit of deafness to leave her. When Branham snapped his fingers the little girl began to hear immediately, and in that same moment, Osborn, sitting in the audience, felt flooded with the power of God while an inner voice whispered, "This is what you should be doing." T.L. Osborn began holding crusades that very year.

After attending a William Branham crusade in Arkansas, a preacher's kid named O.L. Jaggers launched his ministry. Jaggers, who before it was all over would end up being a pretty controversial fellow, eventually founded the New World Church in Los Angeles and launched a national radio ministry.

In 1947, an Assemblies of God pastor named Jack Coe bought a large tent and began holding healing crusades across the country. It was the typical story. Coe was an orphan, raised in poverty, who had an early personal healing experience. He drew big crowds, was unbelievably bold, and saw many miracles.

And in 1947, two new evangelists launched their ministry in Oklahoma. One was a low-key, former Southern Baptist minister by the name of Kenneth Hagin. He would not command a great following during the height of the healing revival, but in the 1960's and 70's, when the charismatic renewal began in the Catholic church and within the rest of traditional Christianity, Hagin's experience and lifelong study of the supernatural would make him an indispensable teacher to many of a new generation.

Oh yes, the other Oklahoma evangelist to launch a new ministry in 1947 was a young Pentecostal Holiness preacher by the name of Oral Roberts. He had finally awakened from his seven months of prayer and fasting that he had begun the year before. All in all, it had been a busy year.

How did Oral Roberts get started?

It was the same formula with some minor twists. Roberts grew up in a preacher's home in Oklahoma. They were members of the Pentecostal Holiness denomination, and they were poor. He was the fifth boy in the family and born in 1918. There is some indication that the Roberts family was a little bit more liberal than some in their denomination. Oral was allowed to play on the high school basketball team at a time when many Pentecostals frowned on such "worldliness."

It was in the middle of a game when Roberts collapsed, and they eventually discovered that he had tuberculosis. Young Oral Roberts was prayed for by a traveling evangelist and was apparently healed—and not only of the tuberculosis. He had a problem of stuttering, and when the traveling evangelist prayed, that left as well. Roberts was 17 years old. He immediately began his ministry.

At age 17?

Right. Such an early ministry was not really that uncommon in Pentecostal circles. The important thing was to have the call of God on your life, not a degree from a university. Pentecostals distrusted formal education. And seminaries, with their newly imported German theologies that questioned the fundamentals of Christianity, were the most distrusted of

all. For 11 years Roberts preached in small Pentecostal Holiness churches across Oklahoma and Texas, even temporarily trying his hand at pastoring. By 1947, he was frustrated. Oral Roberts went into seclusion,
prayer, and fasting. The rest is history.

Was this the turning point for him, something that catapulted his ministry forward?

That very first year, Roberts was able to use the Branham formula
and put together a "union meeting" with three Pentecostal churches in
Muskogee, Oklahoma. It was not a large event by any means, but during
the services there was a pretty remarkable testimony of healing from a
young polio victim. Roberts just took the braces off the kid, declared her
healed, and she walked.

The real turning point, however, was probably Roberts' decision to
publish a magazine. It is a story similar to that of Aimee Semple McPherson. Before 1947 ended, Oral Roberts had launched a new publication
called *The Healing Waters*, which reported on the Muskogee meeting and
introduced a new book written by the evangelist. Before the year was
over, Oral Roberts had stepped into the gap created by William Branham's temporary "retirement" and had assumed the leadership of the
healing movement.

And the magazine was a big part of that?

Absolutely. No question about it. The Branham ministry and all of
the legends and stories that followed in its wake had helped create a
tremendous hunger for the reality of the gospel and for the supernatural manifestation of the Holy Spirit. But where was it happening? Where
could one find it? What was its schedule? How could one get plugged in?

Many felt some disappointment with their local church. Some local
pastors were a bit intimidated by what was happening. The miracles in
the Branham services were almost an indictment against them. Why
weren't such miracles happening in their own ministry? It was easier to
become defensive and critical than it was to face up to the fact that there
was more of God's power available and that there was, perhaps, even
more to learn.

Then, there was the attitude of the people. Jesus said that a prophet
is without honor in his own land. It was easier to believe in some evangelist, from some distant place, than it was to seek healing in your own church.

Gordon Lindsay's magazine, *The Voice of Healing*, with its accounts of William Branham, T.L. Osborn, William Freeman, Jack Coe, and others, was one common denominator for these masses of people. Oral Robert's magazine, *The Healing Waters*, quickly became another one.

It's interesting how the printed page has such impact. It's true in politics and economics as well.

The Pentecostal Evangel really called the great Assemblies of God denomination into being. It invited its readers to come to a convention in Hot Springs, Arkansas, and the fellowship was begun. *The Voice of Healing* really led and shaped the healing movement in America, and later, *The Logos Journal* became the common denominator for the charismatic renewal, much as Steven Strang's *Charisma* magazine does today.

In 1949, William Freeman finally started his own publication, *The Healing Messenger*. And in 1950, Jack Coe launched *The Herald of Healing*. And almost all the new healing evangelists eventually got into radio, but no one ever approached the size and scale of the Oral Roberts ministry. By the time he left the gate in 1947, no one ever caught up.

When did he get his tent?

That started right away. In 1948, he already had one of the largest tents of its kind in existence, and he was touring America. The tent gave an evangelist some control. It was often hard to find auditoriums that were big enough, especially in rural America where the Pentecostal movement was flourishing. Eventually, Oral Roberts' tent seated more than 12,000, which by any standards, even today, is just enormous. Still, he never totally abandoned the auditoriums and coliseums. There were many large union meetings in the cities, and in later years, he began using the tent less and less.

There was some debate about who had the largest tent?

Oh, I remember very well all the debates. Jack Coe supposedly ordered a tent slightly larger than Roberts so that he could claim that distinction. It was all rather comical, but Oral Roberts never got into any of that. He stayed calm, above the fray. He let the little dogs snap at his heels. He had no reason to comment on such issues.

In 1955, he launched a television ministry, and after that, he was off into the stratosphere. His magazine, which as you know was renamed *The Abundant Life*, then had a circulation of one million. That was his fund-raising base. To put that into perspective, the Republican National

Committee at the peak of its fund-raising success with Ronald Reagan as
President, had only one million active donors.

**Over the years, so much has been written and said about Oral
Roberts' organizational talent and his business acumen. Was
that an early source of criticism? Did some feel he was less spiritual for employing secular methods—especially in the wake of
the William Branham mysticism?**

Actually, it was a welcome relief. Oral Roberts was strong in exactly the ways that William Branham was weak. Roberts was organized. If
he said that he was coming to town, you could count on it. Eventually,
the advance work on a crusade began at least a year in advance.

Oral Roberts was a strong preacher. His sermons became best-
selling books to other ministers, who respected his theological consis-
tency and his clear style.

He was a better politician. He made the work of organizing the local
pastors into an art. For example, Roberts took up an offering for all the
participating ministers in his large crusades, and in that atmosphere of
faith and excitement, the offerings were often larger, even after they
were divided, than many pastors had ever received before. Give him
credit; he was a giver. There was always a big breakfast or luncheon that
was free for the local pastors.

But you're right. I suppose the biggest difference between Branham
and Roberts was Roberts' ability as a businessman. He knew how to manage money. Of course, Branham had huge offerings. People were excited and there were great miracles, so at times they had more money than
they knew what to do with. But during the lean months, the Branham
organization would suddenly just dry up. It just wasn't managed.

And throughout all the years, as financially successful as the Oral
Roberts ministry was, there was never a question about integrity. For one
thing, Roberts gave all the cooperating ministers and churches a complete financial accounting of every dime spent. The amounts of the
offerings were publicly announced. The books were open. It was very
honest. Unfortunately, this wasn't the case with many who followed.

**And yet, to many of the new generation, Oral Roberts is
remembered as saying that God might "take him home" if he
didn't meet his overseas missions budget.**

To those of us who know him, it is a great irony. He was always
extremely careful. He went the extra mile. There were always very careful
explanations that a person's healing or answer to prayer could not be

bought by an offering. There was even a strict time limit of three minutes placed on the taking of an offering.

In some respects, it seems as if the William Branham ministry inspired and gave birth to many of the new healing evangelists, but most of them soon came to copy the style of Oral Roberts.

If William Branham was humble, then Oral Roberts came off as confident, as a leader. It wasn't that one was wrong and the other was right. They were different. Looking back on it, one can appreciate both men.

Some of the evangelists who followed Oral Roberts took his confidence or boldness to an extreme. In fact, that would be an understatement. Some were egotistical and cocky. And some took organizing to an extreme. Everything was formulized. You knew what to expect. Audiences were manipulated. "Results" became more important than people. It made some long for the humility and genuineness of the Branham crusades, and for the mysticism as well. Everything was seemingly new then. You never knew quite what to expect.

So, there should be a genuine appreciation for the contributions of both men.

It's hard to distinguish between this early ministry of Oral Roberts and the public persona of today. Obviously his ministry has evolved.

That's right. To understand Oral Roberts during the height of the healing movement, you have to completely wipe out any impressions of Oral Roberts as you know him today. It was a different time in his life, a different ministry, and it was a special time within Christianity. God was awakening the message of healing, and He was using Oral Roberts to do it.

There was much more mystique about Oral Roberts then. Today, he is overexposed. We have seen him for years on television, and we have seen him in a relaxed conversational way, which is what the medium of television demands.

The crusade atmosphere was something altogether different. There was real anticipation. There was the long wait, with all the anxiety about whether you or your loved one would be prayed for or even get a seat. There was a time of worship, with beautiful music, and there were thousands of fellow worshipers instead of the usual small crowd at your local congregation. There was a great soloist or sometimes a visiting celebrity. When Oral Roberts finally appeared, you had been waiting for hours. You hung on every word. He was different too. He had probably come from a time of prayer and maybe even fasting. He had a sense of the supernatural about him. And when the praying for the sick began, it was electric.

When there was an apparent miracle or answer to prayer, you could feel a sense of awe and humility before God. It just seemed to sweep over the audience. The faces of people who had come as skeptics would suddenly cloud over with a worried expression: *Did that happen? Did that really happen?*

I know this is a crass question, but were there any discussions backstage about the percentage of people who were actually healed?

Bob Daniels, who was Oral Robert's soloist for years, tells about a flight back to Tulsa after a crusade. He was onboard the ministry plane with Bob DeWeese, Lee Braxton, Bob Fulton, and the Oral Roberts team. According to Bob Daniels, they got into a discussion about who was actually physically healed, and Oral made the statement that in his opinion about ten percent were actually healed. The others probably just got a good blessing, which was also a wonderful thing.

Ten percent is actually pretty impressive—at least from a natural perspective.

You are absolutely right. Considering that you are dealing with everything from diabetes to cancer, a doctor would love those odds. But it would have been a shock to the audiences. Their faith was high. They wanted everybody to get healed.

Was there an effort to verify what had happened?

There were no records or verifications at first. But within time, Roberts saw the importance of that, and quite an effort was made. There is no doubt that there were many miracles.

Bob Daniels, his soloist, went on to work for Kathryn Kuhlman, and he eventually came on board my team. He was not a traditional Pentecostal and still clung to his Southern Baptist upbringing, but he came away from his crusade experiences very much a believer in healing. He tells the story of a friend in Washington, D.C., named Pat Wiggins. Bob Daniels and Pat Wiggins had worked in Washington together. Wiggins had assisted with the first religious telecast in America. On Sunday evenings, they had held services in the downtown Congregationalist Church. Wiggins was a Georgia Tech graduate, a tall, strapping, handsome fellow, six-foot-two, 230 pounds. The young people loved him.

About ten years later, Daniels was in the middle of an Oral Roberts' crusade in Orlando, when he got a message to meet a friend offstage. Well, there in the shadows was an emaciated figure that probably weighed about 90 pounds and was propped up in a wheelchair. He was drooling, and his head was rolling around. He slobbered as he spoke.

"H-e-l-l-o B-o-b." It was Pat Wiggins. He had an acute case of multiple sclerosis. Everything that could go wrong with a person's nervous system seemed to be going wrong with his. In his current state, he was vegetating. There was no hope. He was almost gone.

Now, here's the interesting part. Wiggins didn't really want to go to the services. He had no faith whatsoever that God would heal him or that God even *could* heal him. Some friends, who were taking care of him, were believers. They had either read the stories in Oral Roberts' magazine, *Abundant Life*, or they had seen the television programs, and they were insistent. Wiggins was totally dependent on them, so there was nothing he could do. Finally, Oral Roberts laid his hand on this frail, dying body, saying, "In Jesus' name, be healed"—and that was the end of that.

A year later, in another town and in another crusade, Pat Wiggins showed up and was dramatically changed from when he had last seen Roberts. He had doctors' affidavits, X-rays, the works. He had even begun giving his testimony and preaching in churches across the country.

We have thousands of Oral Roberts' original magazines here in the archives, and they are loaded with stories of this nature, one after the other. It was a tremendous phenomenon, and it touched thousands of lives.

Roberts didn't encourage the so-called "falling under the power" phenomenon.

No, that wasn't a characteristic of his services. But it did happen from time to time, never disappearing entirely. That phenomenon would eventually come back strong with Kathryn Kuhlman.

You talk about music. When there are moments of renewal within Christianity, they are always accompanied by a wave of

new music. And then it seems that, within time, congregations sing those songs into the ground until they lose all meaning or freshness. Did that kind of phenomenon occur?

Yes. And if I mention the popular songs of that time, the average churchgoers of today would groan because, just as you said, they have been sung into the ground, and they have lost their freshness.

In Branham's meetings the audiences often sang "All Things Are Possible, Only Believe." When it was new, it was a powerful, soft, haunting melody that would stay with you for months after the crusade. In the Roberts' meetings, they often sang "Where the Healing Waters Flow," and later an upbeat theme song, "God Is a Good God." These songs took head-on the cynical question, "If God loves me, why am I sick?"

Bob Daniels had a compassion for people and his deep, clear, baritone voice, resonating out across an audience of thousands of people, set just the right mood to introduce the speaker.

Was there a conscious manipulation of the audiences by some of these evangelists? In that sense, was the music used?

Very often there was a beautiful sense of the presence of God. When that would happen, emotions would run high. Sometimes there would be weeping, for example. At that moment, when the audience would break into singing, they would ride that emotional wave. It would be beautiful. It was a group experience that is very hard to describe; those crowds experienced an awareness of God's love that would haunt them for the rest of their lives.

At other times, for some reason or another, there wouldn't be that same group feeling. The interesting thing is that everyone could tell the difference. The music was the same. The speaker would appeal to the same emotions, but afterward when people compared notes, they could all tell the difference. So, more and more, evangelists would try to seek ways to create that sense of the presence of God. They examined what had worked and why.

Incidentally, this was not something contrived solely by the evangelist. He wasn't trying to put something over on the people. The audiences themselves would participate in this. For example, some may even try to weep or try to respond emotionally in a sincere effort to recapture something they had experienced the week before or sometime in the past year.

Even so, even if the evangelists and audiences sometimes had to stretch to hang onto the revival, there is still an interesting point that we must consider: *You can't fake something that doesn't exist.* An artist can copy a master, but if there were no master, there could be no faked copy. The Holy Spirit did really blow through the midst of the healing revival. The latter attempts to hang onto it and recreate it may have been absurd and ugly and phony, but that only underscores the fact that the original was a thing of beauty.

Understand though that these evangelists weren't Harvard graduates. Most of them were barely high school graduates. They were basically uneducated, poor people. They weren't psychologists. But they had been given great secrets that had been hidden from biblical scholars and Church authorities for years. They were just trying their best. It really is so typical of how God works. After all, this is the same God who chose a manger full of animals and manure to be the place of birth for His Son.

You've mentioned Jack Coe a couple of times. Tell me more about him.

In the 1950's, by any standard, Jack Coe was one of the giants of the healing revival. He had a huge tent that rivaled the one Oral Roberts traveled with. His crusade crowds were tremendous. Coe was big, bold, and boisterous, and he often shocked people with his daring, almost reckless faith. I remember people telling me that they would leave a Jack Coe meeting shaking their heads in amazement.

It's a great story. Like so many others we've talked about, Jack had a lot to overcome. His early home life was troubled and difficult. His father was addicted to alcohol and gambling. Jack used to talk about the time his father's gambling debts were so big that they lost all their furniture, and finally their house. Often they had nothing to eat and had to go to bed hungry.

By the time Jack was 17 years old, he had spent eight years in an orphanage. Then came a battle with alcoholism and an almost fatal sickness brought on by his incessant drinking. It was his near-death experience that finally brought him to his knees in repentance. Sensing the call of God to the ministry, Jack attended Southwestern Bible Institute, an Assemblies of God Bible college.

So, was Jack Coe considered a more traditional Pentecostal?

Far from it. Coe was ordained an Assemblies of God minister in 1944, but it was a shaky relationship at best. Coe's fierce independence always annoyed the hierarchy in Springfield. In 1947, he rented his first tent and started his own magazine to publicize his meetings. He opened a children's home near Dallas, Texas, in 1950—a project remembering his own days as an orphan. But the final blow came in 1952 when Jack decided to build an independent congregation in Dallas, Texas. He was expelled from the Assemblies of God in 1953. Coe simply held to his independent ways, and in 1954 he opened the Dallas Revival Center. It became one of the largest churches in Dallas. Just about every well-known evangelist preached there.

Why didn't we hear more about his ministry?

Well, Coe was highly controversial and generally regarded as an extremist by most traditional Pentecostals. He dogmatically opposed the medical profession and preached that people were looking to the wrong source for healing when they consulted doctors. Coe loved to make extreme statements, and he may have been playing to his audience with such controversy, but his position against doctors was typical of his approach. He has been described as "sometimes saucy, sometimes angry, sometimes flippant, sometimes humble, but always nervy." He thrived on controversy and generated more than his share of it with his pulpit tactics. He seemed to always enjoy a fight. But he was fearless. He looked for the hardest cases, and God honored his daring faith.

His sudden, premature death in late 1956 brought an end to his powerful presence on the healing scene. Gordon Lindsay wrote this in his obituary: "Jack Coe, lovable, impulsive, bold in spirit yet tender-hearted, beloved of thousands, though not without bitter enemies." I think that statement pretty well sums up my impressions of Jack Coe as well.

Growing up in a Pentecostal home, and a preacher's home at that, I met many of these evangelists and sat under their ministries. Of course, as a child, one doesn't pay much attention to where the evangelist came from and how he got started. Tell me about some of these men, Richard Vinyard, for example.

If you remember, Richard Vinyard was a Damon Runyan type of character; he was rough and handsome. In 1948, when William Branham came to Kansas City, Vinyard was a local Assembly of God pastor. Vinyard was moved by what happened and became a little disappointed with his own ministry as a result. After Branham left town, he followed the same pattern of many others; he set himself aside to pray and fast until he was awakened one morning with a clear message that he had been given a ministry of healing. He announced it to his church. There were some immediate miracles, and he hit the road. Richard Vinyard had some spectacular meetings over the years and was prominently featured in *The Voice of Healing* magazine.

I mentioned David Nunn as the young World War II veteran who came back home as an alcoholic. He was converted in 1946 and began preaching in the Assemblies of God a few years later. Nunn finally felt a call to a healing ministry and had almost immediate success. Some of the stories and testimonials were dramatic—blind eyes opened, for example. David Nunn became a close partner to Gordon Lindsay in the work of *The Voice of Healing*, and for a long time he became their radio evangelist.

What about Velmer Gardner?

Velmer Gardner was a very bright man. Although he only had a Bible school education, he was very, very sharp. He began as an Assemblies of God minister, but after attending an Oral Roberts crusade in 1949, he came away inspired to launch his own healing ministry.

No one could hold an audience like Velmer Gardner. He was just a great storyteller. And he was perhaps the best fund-raiser in the *Voice of Healing*. Actually, that became a bit of a problem for him. Since he was so good at raising money, he was often the one who would get the assignment, and over a period of time, the reputation backfired on him.

Toward the end of the revival, Gardner got a lot of criticism, with charges of exaggerating his sermon illustrations or using pressure tactics in taking up an offering. But there were remarkable healings, and his powerful and convincing sermons gave faith to thousands of people.

And W.V. Grant?

Grant was an important leader primarily because of his writing. He turned out dozens of small books even though he was not a great intellect. His magazine, *Voice of Deliverance*, eventually reached a circulation of two million. For a while, Grant served as the vice president of the *Voice of Healing* organization.

Tell me about Morris Cerullo.

Cerullo was one of the youngest of the *Voice of Healing* evangelists, and at this writing, he is still going strong, albeit with a changed ministry. In 1990, he bought the old PTL television network, and he briefly telecast from there. He's definitely on the mystical side. Cerullo has this deep, husky, dramatic voice, and in a style reminiscent of Bill Branham, he talks to his audience about what God is revealing to him.

Like Jack Coe, Morris Cerullo was an orphan. In Cerullo's case, he was reared in an Orthodox Jewish orphanage where one of the women workers passed him a New Testament. The woman got fired, but when Cerullo was older, he sought her out and converted to Christianity. Morris Cerullo was one of several *Voice of Healing* evangelists who eventually took the movement international. He had some spectacular success, filling soccer stadiums all over the Third World.

For many years he conducted an annual *Deeper Life Conference* in San Diego. He would bring in some of the outstanding national church leaders from around the world, along with some of the people who had experienced remarkable healings. At a time when the revival was clearly moving out of the United States, it was Cerullo's way of bringing a taste of it back from some of the big crusades overseas.

The ministry of Oral Roberts became so famous and transcendent that it's easy to forget how powerful some of these other ministries were.

You could pick any one of them and fill a book with stories of healings and unexplainable phenomenas. They are all very remarkable biographies. Gayle Jackson, for example, was featured in a big spread in *Look* Magazine. Tommy Hicks was a personal friend of several Latin American heads of state. He dined with them in their homes and prayed for their close, personal friends. There are some remarkable stories.

When you visited in any one of these crusades, you had the feeling that it was the most important place on earth in that moment. You felt as if God Himself was making it His current headquarters. What had once only taken place in the ministry of a Smith Wigglesworth or a Charles Price was now multiplied hundreds and hundreds of times over. On any given night, it was happening in a hundred places.

Did people get jaded? Did they take it all for granted?

Yes, they did, very much so. A miracle ceases to become a miracle when it continually reoccurs. The mind is temporarily stunned, but it says, "Wait, wait, I'll figure this out." And, sure enough, given enough time we can rationalize anything away. There was no way that it could be sustained without destroying it. Looking back, one can understand why it had to pass. Remember the quote I referred to earlier? Jesus said the work of the Spirit is like the wind (see Jn. 3:8). We don't know where it comes from, and we don't know where it goes, but we know that it has passed by. Well, it goes and it moves. That is part of its nature.

Talk to me about the relationship between all these evangelists and the outside world. How were the leaders of organized religion responding? Was the media alarmed?

There were fireworks immediately.

It was one thing for highly educated traditional churchmen, such as Presbyterian Edward Irving, to teach and practice divine healing. That was less controversial, even a bit avant garde and trendy. But when the healing revival really broke open in America, the evangelists were poor and uneducated and so were their Pentecostal audiences. Some critics may have felt the need to protect these people. You always have that, especially among persons in government and leadership: "We're smarter than you so we are going to protect you from yourself. We will decide what you can and cannot believe."

The newspapers alternated between open ridicule and hostile attacks. But the publicity only added to the excitement and brought out the crowds. Of all the evangelists, A.A. Allen was the best at playing off of this negative publicity to fill his crusades. Even when the healing revival had waned, Allen could provoke a front-page story when he came to town. And if someone really believed that he had experienced a healing, nothing the journalists wrote could take it away.

The big event in 1956 was the arrest of Jack Coe on charges of practicing medicine without a license. He was in the middle of a Miami crusade when it happened, and for believers across the country, this was big, big stuff. I mean, we had been reading the Bible all our lives. The disciples were constantly arrested. And when they were set free, they went right back to healing the sick and preaching the gospel. This was just like the Bible.

Some historians of the movement talk about the event as if it were a setback, but it was just the opposite. It galvanized the true believers and even granted the healing movement some authenticity. After all, Jesus had talked about persecution and warned His disciples that they would be thrown into prison.

All evangelicals were students of eschatology and held a belief that the end of the world would be accompanied by persecution of the believers. The healing evangelists were all specialists on the subject. It seemed like organized governmental persecution was beginning to happen. Instead of great fear, there was an excitement, a feeling that it was all real, that it was all going to happen, but that God would be with us as He had promised. Jack Coe was a hero.

What happened?

Well, of course, after listening to testimony from ministers, theologians, and people who claimed that they were healed, the judge threw it out of court. It had no business there in the first place.

In his book, *All Things Are Possible*, David Harrell, Jr., refers to a statement made that very year by the American Medical Association, saying that "all miracle cures were the result of suggestion, spontaneous remission, or wrong diagnosis."

When you think about it, that position is just as anti-intellectual and anti-scientific as the position of the more radical healing evangelists themselves, who felt that it was sacrilegious to question spiritual things. If, in fact, the A.M.A. statement was really believed, namely that there were miracle cures through suggestion, then why didn't someone study the revival? A "miracle cure" is still a "miracle cure" to the patient. The patient doesn't care how it happened. Why was there no research to determine the percentages of spontaneous remission from those who prayed for healing compared to a norm group that didn't? If it was all misdiagnosis, why was there not a major outcry over the huge numbers of misdiagnosis?

This wasn't about truth. It was about money and social standing. Many doctors were alarmed by the teaching of the more radical evangelists who suggested that people who received medical treatment were lacking in faith. And, in fairness, it made them understandably angry if a patient suffered or even died because he or she refused medical treatment. Oral Roberts and many of the more responsible leaders urged their audiences to get checked out by their doctors and taught that God and medicine could work together.

But then again, no one wanted to admit that these uneducated Pentecostals were on to anything. There was no real, objective, outside inquiry into what was going on. That same year, 1956, A.A. Allen was arrested and convicted in California for operating a business without a license. It was just pure harassment. A higher court overturned it, but not before Allen spent thousands of dollars on attorney fees.

Incidentally, another positive from the Jack Coe incident was a renewed sense of accountability on the part of the healing evangelists.

They were on the alert. They had to learn the law. They had to be conscious of how they worded their literature and the nature of their claims. It was really healthy—scary, but healthy.

How were the leaders of organized religion responding?

Well, that's where the real battle was fought. Most of the doctors, local sheriffs, or publishers who harassed the Pentecostals were in fact members of other Christian denominations that were in bitter disagreement with the Pentecostals over doctrine.

In fairness, much of that conflict was also over money. When the healing crusade came to town, often the churches were emptied. Many of the leaders in traditional Christian churches were horrified. How could people who had been in their church for so many years be so easily swayed? Many actually left their old congregations and joined a local Pentecostal church. The crusades had huge budgets, and consequently, they raised lots of money to pay for everything. Churches were furious.

Of course, some in the Church of Christ and the Baptist churches were genuinely offended over the doctrine of divine healing. They would openly attack the revival. Some took out full-page advertisements in the newspapers, warning people to stay away. Of course, this only heightened the excitement and drew attention to the event. But there were also constant testimonies of people from those very denominations claiming a healing. So, that kind of open opposition didn't really hurt.

One of the interesting stories to come out of the revival occurred in Houston, Texas, in 1950. A local Baptist pastor challenged someone from the William Branham crusade team to debate the Scriptures on the subject of divine healing. It was a lively debate, widely covered in the press, and of course, it swelled the audience for the crusade. That night while Branham preached, numerous people claimed to have seen a luminous halo appear over his head. When a photograph came back clearly showing the white blur, it caused quite a commotion. Skeptics came back night after night, trying to see if some reflection of light had caused it. The film negative was scrutinized. Old friends in Indiana said, "That's nothing new. It happened when he was born, and it happened at a Baptist baptismal service years later."

In fact, all this made a lot of people nervous.

What about the Pentecostal churches? How were they reacting to the revival?

The leaders grew restless and then finally hostile.

The great secret to the William Branham meetings and the key to the successful ministries of Oral Roberts and all who followed were the "union meetings." The miracles in Branham's services transcended the petty doctrinal issues, and for a while, the Pentecostals in a given community would unite to help sponsor his crusade. There were dozens of little congregations from dozens of little denominations. When they got together, the Pentecostals were often quite surprised at their own strength.

But as time wore on and the numbers of evangelists and meetings began to proliferate, the churches became drained. They reached a saturation point, similar to the experience of the televangelists of the 1980's. There was only one dollar to go around, and it had to be sliced in thousands of different ways by thousands of different ministries. Evangelists became more sensational. The offerings became more dramatic. There were all kinds of attempts to keep things under control. Oral Roberts had his firm rule that only three minutes could be used for the offering. But the mistrust between the denominational leaders and many of the various evangelists grew.

Some of these denominational leaders were more gifted as administrators and politicians than as preachers. They may have felt a bit intimidated and nervous about the large followings that the healing evangelists were attracting. Sometimes they may have responded just out of jealousy. Whatever the reason, when the numbers shifted and there were more Pentecostals troubled by the excesses in the healing revival than those who supported it, these church leaders reacted quickly.

Jack Coe was one of the first to go. He was dismissed from the Assemblies of God denomination in 1953, even before his big arrest in Miami. He hadn't committed adultery, preached a false doctrine, or misused money. But he was out. The Assemblies of God leaders used a disingenuous method that, at the time, may have violated their own by-laws. They said that they weren't kicking him out; they were just not going to renew him. According to their own by-laws, in order to kick him out they would have had to give him a trial and would have had to prove something. But they could grant or deny fellowship to anyone who wasn't already in without a trial. When his annual credentials with the Assemblies expired, they declared him out, and thereafter, they refused to let him in again. This procedure was soon formalized as the accepted method to purge the denomination.

Soon the Assemblies of God passed resolutions saying that their churches could no longer have non-Assemblies preachers in their pulpits.

It was a rigid exclusivism brought on by the growing tension between the healing movement and the denomination. David Nunn was just an Assembly of God pastor when he was hauled in on the carpet for having a *Voice of Healing* speaker in his pulpit. Nunn then left the denomination to start his own ministry.

Velmer Gardner withdrew in protest. W.V. Grant eventually left. All of them eventually left. There just wasn't room for them. Oral Roberts was too big for the little Pentecostal Holiness denomination to kick around, so he didn't have to go through that humiliation. Yet the Assemblies of God hierarchy even got some licks in on him. When he started his new Oral Roberts University, they kicked out anyone with Assemblies of God credentials who taught at the school. I guess they felt ORU competed with their own colleges.

There is no doubt that some of the healing evangelists brought on their own problems, but the answer lay in working out some guidelines and defining the rules. Gordon Lindsay was working very hard to that end. Your [Doug Wead's] own father, Roy Wead, who was an Assembly of God leader, was trying to bring about a resolution from the denominational side. But the hotheads on both sides prevailed.

From the perspective of the healing evangelist, I feel that vengeful denominational leaders were seizing upon the mistakes and controversial behavior of a few, to wipe out all the others, including some very humble and honest ministers who were acting in good faith, trying to meet the denominational standards. When they began to catch on to the fact that the denominational bureaucracy had already ruled against them and were going to kick them out anyway, even if a situation had to be manufactured, some were deeply hurt. This was dishonest. It wasn't Christian. It was petty. And it had the unfortunate consequence of further radicalizing the healing movement. Now, there were no restraints. It was not the denominations' finest hour.

And then there was A.A. Allen?

Yes. Well, that's quite a story in itself.

Chapter Five

Evangelist on a Hot Tin Roof—
From the Tent to the Airwaves

A.A. Allen

His name was actually Asa Alonso Allen, which may explain why he just used his initials. Allen was born on March 27, 1911. Both of his parents were drunkards. He was raised in total poverty; his first pair of shoes were bought for him by a total stranger.

I can remember Allen saying his mother was the meanest woman he ever knew. His parents made homebrew behind the shack where they lived. When his mother was pregnant with him, she was a very heavy drinker.

His parents would make him drink the homebrew until he was in a drunken stupor. Then they would laugh at him; this was their form of entertainment. Even as a baby, his mother would fill his baby bottle with liquor to keep him from crying. This was how he went to sleep every night.

At a very early age, his mother would send him out on the street to sing and dance as the crowd would toss him coins.

His parents were constantly fighting, throwing objects at each other and threatening each other with weapons. Finally, when he was four years old, his mother took him and his sister to Carthage, Missouri. Soon his mother remarried.

But the problems were just as bad or worse. His mother and step-father were constantly in drunken rages. The children would be so afraid that they would run out of the house, afraid to go back in, thinking that they would be killed. By the time Allen was six years old, he was carrying tin buckets of beer home from the saloon for his stepfather.

I remember Allen saying he and his brother grew up with the taste of liquor. One of his brothers died when he was a little boy. The other died a drunkard. He would say, "My father filled a drunken grave." His mother finally quit drinking by the time he was grown.

Several times Allen ran away from home. The first time, he was only 11 years old; the second time, he was 14. He hopped freight cars and hitched all over the South picking cotton, working in gins, and digging ditches. He eventually ended up in jail for stealing.

In 1934, Allen had a conversion experience in a rural Methodist church, which for all practical purposes was a Pentecostal congregation. Almost all the church members had experienced the baptism of the Holy Spirit, but the local Methodist bishop hadn't yet found out about it and hadn't yet come in to clean it all out. Within a few years, A.A. Allen was traveling as an itinerant Assemblies of God evangelist. He had married Lexie by then, and they had four children. It was not an easy life. He used to tell us young preachers that his first revival brought in the grand sum of 35 cents.

In 1947, just as the healing revival started to hit, A.A. Allen accept-ed the pastorate of an Assemblies of God church in Corpus Christi, Texas. When someone handed him a copy of *The Voice of Healing* maga-zine, he was unimpressed, dismissing it all as extremism. But within a few years, he began to hear more and more about the healing revival. In 1949, he and a Baptist pastor named Lester Rollof slipped into an Oral Roberts crusade in Dallas, Texas. The tent was packed, but one of the ushers recognized them. All the visiting ministers were sitting on the platform, and so they were taken up and seated on the last row. They were the last two seats in the tent.

That was the turning point for Allen. He talked about it even years later. There was a very real sense of the power of God in the meeting. The miracles of healing seemed very genuine, and he found himself in an experience similar to that of T.L. Osborn in the Bill Branham cru-sade. Allen felt God speaking to him to launch his own healing ministry.

You know, there is something in the whole history of this movement that just isn't coming through. There are so many

examples of ministers such as A.A. Allen who were inspired by their experience at the crusade of another evangelist. How do you explain that duplication? Why isn't it happening today? For example, why don't people leave a Don Stewart meeting or a Benny Hinn meeting and go out and launch their own similar ministry?

I think what we're missing when we talk about these services is just how beautiful and powerful the atmosphere really was. We get glimpses of it today, but not to the same degree. You could even ask the question, why don't people visit an Oral Roberts service today and leave like A.A. Allen did in 1949? All I can say is that it was a very special time. People like Allen, Osborn, and Vinyard were all very deeply moved by what they saw and felt. It was life-changing.

And were there crowds right away for Allen?

Almost. After a crusade in Oakland, California, he sent in his first reports to *The Voice of Healing*. There were hundreds of reported healings.

How did the healing line evolve? What was that all about?

There were so many who came for healing that you had to organize them into a line. As the crowds grew, you had to pass out healing cards, which were sort of like free tickets. If you didn't do that the people would just rush the stage. Many were desperate. But with an organized healing line, the evangelist could call for the pink cards or the blue cards. It was just a way to help make it work. Also, there were so many people who came from such distances. The healing card assured them that they would not be forgotten, that eventually they would be prayed for.

Then we learned that many of the people coming for healing were not even believers. They had no conversion experience; they just wanted to be healed. Others came who didn't understand the role they had to play; they didn't know the importance of their own faith in the process. They had to be taught that Jesus was the healer, not the evangelist. The evangelist was only there to pray in Jesus' name. Rather than give the same instructions over and over in the middle of each service to people who had been going to church all their lives, the evangelist and his team would meet earlier in the afternoon with those people who wanted a healing. They could then have a time of teaching and go over the basics.

Bob DeWeese conducted these so-called "faith clinics" for Oral Roberts. Some said he was a better preacher than Roberts. When his own ministry took off, A.A. Allen had R.W. Shambach and Kent Rogers conducting such clinics, and during the 1960's, I was conducting them too.

These afternoon teaching sessions gave the evangelist a chance to actually talk to the people who were praying for a miracle. What was their attitude? Did they really have faith? Now, William Branham didn't do that. When he prayed for someone publicly, he had never seen that person before in his life. And Oral Roberts usually had other advance people help instruct and prepare those who wanted healing. But A.A. Allen loved people so much that he liked to actually see them eye to eye.

Later, in the evening service that night, the Holy Spirit would direct Allen, and he would start calling some of the special cases to the front. He was looking for one or two with great faith. If they received a miracle, then it would spread like electricity and many others would follow. This happened night after night.

And the miracles were real?

They were real, and they were public. Young, ten-year-old Marshall Prince, the polio poster child, was healed. He had been in braces since he was two years old, and there were many nights that he couldn't sleep because of the pain. One foot was totally withered, but after his healing he was completely normal. He began jumping and running all over the place.

Almost every night in every city, the hospitals would bring out dying patients in ambulances. They would drive right up to the tent and wheel people out on stretchers with attendants nearby.

The hospitals didn't sanction the meetings, did they?

Oh no. These were usually people who had heard about the meetings by word of mouth. Later, more and more came because of the radio broadcasts. They were dying anyway, and so their doctors would give them permission to go. Many, many of them had cancer, and there were many healings.

Incidentally, Allen would never ignore these emergency invalids. He would always pray for everyone. On his way to the platform, he would often stop by the invalid section and tell the nurses, "Now, when I call for you, bring this person right up to the platform."

And when there were healings, did the ministry document them?

The Voice of Healing was pretty strict. They wanted signed eyewitnesses to confirm everything and they published the stories complete with real names and cities. This went on for years and years, without ever any charges of fraud or misrepresentation. And when Allen started publishing his own *Miracle Magazine*, he ran similar stories month after month.

With my own eyes, I saw God instantly give a woman new skin. It was in the Paramount, California, crusade. They brought a woman in on a stretcher; she was dying of cancer. When Allen pulled the sheet off of her, there was an audible gasp from the ministers on stage. The odor was unbelievable. She was all covered with this ugly thing. Her whole front was a mass of blood, puss, and cancer. The open wound extended from her chest down to her intestines. It was the worst any of us had ever seen, and we had been dealing with dying cancer patients every night for years.

When Allen prayed, the color and texture of that mass up by her chest began to change to that of normal skin. It just kept changing and changing and moving down the body. The wound started to close. Others were standing there looking on. One of our ministers almost fainted. We had all seen healings every night for years, but we had never seen anything like this. When the woman began to see it happening, she jumped up off that stretcher and started shouting, "Thank You, Jesus! Thank You, Jesus!" Everyone was crying.

In typical A.A. Allen style, he ordered out for a hot dog with ketchup and mustard and had the lady eat it right there. The audience was moved, but from their angle, they couldn't have possibly seen just how dramatic it had been. So, there were some pretty powerful moments happening in Allen's meetings. As the stories began to circulate, the crowds grew and so did the people's faith to believe for the impossible.

He bought a tent?

He actually bought William Branham's tent, which was quite a bold step for an evangelist whose first revival had netted him 35 cents. And in 1953, he launched *The Allen Revival Hour*, a radio broadcast that eventually reached across the nation.

Allen was really quite inventive with his radio ministry. He was one of the first to tape record his services and edit them for broadcast. He had one of his trucks remade into a traveling recording studio, which was really quite innovative for that time.

The Allen Revival Hour always opened with his theme song. Listeners would hear: "If you believe you shall receive. There's not a trouble or care the good Lord can't relieve." Then Allen would take you into a service where he would be praying for the sick. He might be cursing a cancer or picking someone up off a stretcher. You could hear the response of the audience and then one of the associates, R.W. Shambach, Kent Rogers, or later, myself, would give the radio audience a description of what was happening. "This woman hasn't taken a step in six years, and she is now walking around this tent. What a miracle! Bible days are here again. Listen to these people praise God." Then Allen would talk to the person to confirm what had happened. Of course, this was old-time radio, which in some ways was much more powerful than television. The listener had no restraints on his or her imagination.

Even though Allen had a relatively late start in the healing revival and even though he was not the first to establish a big radio network, he quickly became the movement's radio champion. He did it by purchasing time on powerful Mexican stations. The airtime was cheap, but the nighttime signals blanketed the southern United States. One could drive old Route 66 and hear A.A. Allen all the way from Chicago to Los Angeles. When one signal faded, another nearby would come in strong.

Many writers have compared A.A. Allen with Jack Coe.

They were both very bold. Like Jack Coe, Allen seemed to look for the hardest cases, the most unlikely to be healed. He went right for the wheelchairs. In fact, the more visible the miracle, the better it would be since that would inspire faith in others. And then Jack Coe and A.A. Allen had huge ministries. After Branham and Roberts, they were the biggest.

In 1956, Jack Coe died. It was diagnosed as polio. This was a shock to many believers, even though all the healing evangelists preached that famous Scripture, "It is appointed unto man once to die, and after that the judgment" (see Heb. 9:27). The message of healing did not guarantee life forever. But Coe was still in his thirties, and it begged the question: Why wasn't he healed? There was a bittersweet irony. Those who visited Jack Coe's crusades remember his theme song: "Though He Slay Me, Yet I'll Trust Him." God took him at 38 years of age.

Shortly after, A.A. Allen bought Jack Coe's mammoth tent. So arguably, technically, Allen ended up with the largest tent of the healing revival. It could seat 12,000.

The thing that so many found controversial about A.A. Allen was the emphasis on demons.

Yeah. You're right. It was very controversial. It did not win him any friends, but it was also very scriptural. The whole molecular structure of the universe is positive and negative. You can't have it one way. You can't say that the New Testament is true, that the supernatural world exists, but only the good parts.

There was a lot of this kind of activity right from the beginning. It was often manifested in William Branham's meetings. Someone would jump up and start shouting or sometimes actually start foaming at the mouth. It could get very rough. Branham would just direct a calm, quiet command, and the person would fall over into a dead faint and be still.

A.A. Allen was really provocative. He seemed to relish such outbursts. He shouted right back at the demon and told it what was going to happen.

But these were people?

These were people. Psychologists would say that they were schizophrenic, that they had split or multiple personalities. Yet in our theology, they were demon possessed. All the spiritual activity of the meeting would stir them up. It was not something that we went looking for. It just happened. Incidentally, it started happening in the ministry of Jesus when He started praying for the sick. Sickness and demonic oppression have some kind of connection.

The criticism is that a preoccupation with demons is unhealthy, that there is a natural fascination that leads to experimentation, which sometimes has unforeseen and tragic consequences. I suppose there is also the fear of "negative suggestion," that by fearing too much one can cause it to happen.

Well, I agree, but there is something even worse, and that is to be trapped into this "demon possessed" situation and have no remedy. As you pointed out, these are people. They are mothers, fathers, children. In some cases, they can't even function. In other cases, whole families were devastated by the situation. Sometimes the person is perfectly normal and then, just when everything is going okay, he can flip out again. Many of these people are very, very poor. They couldn't afford months and years of psychiatric help. And usually in these cases, the psychiatrists can't do anything anyway but just record and study the phenomenas.

In some towns there was a counseling service for that kind of problem. It usually consisted of a psychiatrist and a priest or minister. Very, very often they would refer some of these people to us. They couldn't understand why we had the success rate that we did, but usually it was because they didn't even believe it was demon possession. Yet they knew that we got results, and so they sent the people to us. Allen welcomed it.

In these revival meetings, if someone had that kind of a problem, it would come to the surface very quickly. Some evangelists had the people bodily removed from the service; they couldn't deal with it. Others, such as Branham, had complete and masterful control. He could just say a word and there would be complete obedience. The person controlled by the demon would do exactly what Branham said. And when Branham spoke the word of deliverance, the demon left the person.

I still see it happen frequently in our international crusades. The deliverances are truly wonderful miracles for the family that experiences them. Afterward, the person's entire countenance changes. Sometimes people just collapse they feel so relaxed and exhausted after the experience. Their families are usually weeping with joy and hugging each other.

One of Allen's more celebrated exorcisms involved a young mother who had repeatedly tried to kill her children. During the day she was as sane as you or I. She could pass a whole battery of psychiatric tests. In fact, she had. But something would happen as darkness fell. She would turn violent and start threatening her babies. The family would have her committed, but the authorities would turn around and release her, declaring her to be perfectly normal. The police didn't know what to do. They would sometimes come out and fight with her. She would go after them or her husband with a butcher knife as she tried to get at the kids. She couldn't be sent to prison unless she actually killed somebody, and the family didn't want her to go to prison anyway.

Now, during the daytime, she did the dishes, loved her babies, cooked meals, and conversed normally with her parents, but every night she went berserk. She finally insisted that they lock her up in a barn every evening while this thing would come over her. They could hear her shriek, and curse, and shout out how she was going to kill her babies. It would sometimes go on until dawn, and it was leaving the whole family a wreck.

Finally, they brought her to an A.A. Allen crusade. He didn't miss a beat. He wasn't in the least intimidated. He called for the demon, and although it had successfully hidden itself from psychiatric workers, it immediately manifested itself. Her face became contorted and ugly. Allen talked to it only briefly, and then he commanded it to leave. She was instantly delivered, and it never came back. Years later, that woman was still giving her testimony.

Now, it's easy for you and others to say that A.A. Allen was preoccupied with demons. But where can people like that go today? Today, we take them away from their families, load them up on drugs, and forget about them. If someone like that came into a Baptist or Assemblies of God church of today, we would be embarrassed and pretend that it wasn't really happening. We would call up a hospital, even though the Bible very clearly tells us what to do. So, yes it was controversial, and A.A. Allen suffered because of the controversy. Yet there were people in need, and as the old saying goes, "Somebody's got to do it."

What did you learn about demon possession? How did it happen to people?

It usually happened to people who played around with the occult. Sometimes their parents led them into it. Sometimes it started out as simply with an act, such as playing with a Ouija board. Often, when people went into it deeply, they were led to believe that they would obtain some advantage or power or special knowledge, and at first they would get it. I know of a man who claimed that he had been able to bet on the horses and win. But he eventually went broke. Some so-called witches would come to meetings, claiming that at one time they had incredible powers with leading citizens among their clientele. Yet, once again, their powers would eventually fail them.

That was another lesson I saw over and over again. The mediums and fortune-tellers were usually reduced to poverty before the demon was finished with them. They grew to rely on some special advantage, and then they are betrayed. Such people often become suicidal. Remember when Jesus commanded the demons to leave the man and go into the swine? The swine ran off into the sea and killed themselves. This is the ultimate goal of demonic possession—self-destruction. In foreign countries, we still see demon-possessed people coming, with self-inflicted wounds all over their bodies. Often, there are scars on their wrists where they have tried to end it all. The devil wants to kill them. That's what I believe.

As far as mankind is concerned, there are not two sides in the spirit world—God's side and satan's side. There is only one side, God's side. If you don't have God, you are lost. You have nothing. You are on your own. Don't expect any help because it won't be there.

Do you still practice exorcisms?

Yes. I believe it's a sign that should follow the believer according to Mark 16:17.

Just how common is demon possession?

Well, the answer is, nobody really knows. There are no public studies on it, and who would admit to it anyway? Science and theology define it differently. So it is not easy to come up with any meaningful numbers.

From my personal experience, which is, of course, very subjective, I think it is quite common. I think many people suffer from what we call demon possession and are not even aware of it. In the A.A. Allen meetings, when all that kind of activity was stirred up, it was amazing how many people needed deliverance. Sometimes a visitor, a total unbeliever, would come to a meeting and suddenly begin to manifest a demonic spirit. The friends who came with that person would be shocked.

What would happen?

The person might stand up and start cursing or shouting toward the pulpit. It would be very ugly and frightening. *Hate* is the word that best describes what they were expressing. The air would become filled with the feeling of hate. Of course, Allen would know what was going on, and he would explain it to the audience. He would warn the people that when he cast the demon out of the individual that it would seek someone else to go into and that they had better take the time right then to get their life straight with God. Boy, you never saw people pray like they would at those times. There were no skeptics in the audience then—not one. It was a pretty frightening scene. When it was all over, the person would be as calm and kind and mellow as could be. Of course, the people visiting with him would be shaken.

There is the theory that demon possession was more common in Third World countries because of a lack of education and because of the hold superstition has on the masses.

There is some truth to that. There are some countries in Africa where the national religion is spiritism. Possession is almost a common experience in some tribal ritual celebrations. But in my opinion, it is much more common in the United States than most would believe. Remember that there are degrees of possession. Some individuals are in worse shape than others. I think it may have something to do with spousal abuse and child abuse and violent crime. Serial killers often manifest symptoms of demon possession. Son of Sam claimed that he received his instructions to murder from a barking dog. Also remember that demons know how to lay low. Some of the most violent and cruel of the serial killers manifest an uncanny ability to avoid detection and capture. They could live apparently normal lives for years. Their next-door neighbors would be in shock when the police came in to dig up bodies of the victims.

But in this highly charged spiritual atmosphere of a healing revival, the demons could not stay dormant. They would come quickly to the surface, and A.A. Allen welcomed it. He had complete confidence in such situations. His face would beam. He knew what was going to happen. The demons always obeyed.

Did anything ever go wrong?

Nothing happened during my time with him. There were some stories of things that happened before my time. The old-timers on the staff talked about Indianapolis. Apparently, the crusade was held near a fairgrounds or carnival. A.A. Allen cast out a demon. Everybody was peaceful. Everything was hunky dory, and then a few minutes later, someone from the carnival came bursting into the tent, creating a scene, followed along from behind by concerned friends or family. The demon had apparently left the tent and found someone new at the carnival. Well, this scene repeated itself three or four times in a row. This was new. This was a tough one. Finally, Allen had the whole congregation turn around and get on their knees and pray while he commanded the demon to leave the city. Then, finally, there was peace.

The worst incident happened in Cincinnati. Some demons were tougher than others; no matter how many times Allen would cast the demon out of an individual, the demon would find someone else in the tent, and there would be a new crisis all over again. It just kept going on and on. Of course, the relatives and friends of the newly possessed person were just in shock. This was someone they personally knew, and all of a sudden, here was this weird voice saying these weird things. Even people on the evangelistic team started getting nervous. Allen finally sat everyone down and instructed the people on praying and fasting to get spiritual power and how to resist evil spirits. They resumed the crusade the next night, and everything was cool.

But that was very, very rare. Night after night, year after year, A.A. Allen dealt successfully with whatever came his way in that realm. You asked earlier about what percentage of persons were healed, yet I would say that almost everybody who came for deliverance got it. It was uncanny.

Did it last?

To tell you the truth, we had such faith that we never even questioned that. I suppose we were pretty naive in that regard. But to this day, I firmly believe that such deliverances lasted. The people never wrote for further prayer, nor did any show up again asking for help. Thousands wrote back and told how their life had been changed.

In fact, I can think of just one exception that might just prove the rule. In Los Angeles, the old-timers talked about a woman called "Big Carol." She was delivered, but each time we came back the demons had come back into her. She seemed to relish the attention. Jesus warned about that in the Scriptures. He said that after a deliverance the person must clean up his or her life or the demons would come back worse than ever. The point is this. "Big Carol" was an exception. She had mixed emotions. Sometimes she wanted the demons. Sometimes she wanted to be normal. But tens of thousands of others went on to lead productive lives, never to be bothered by the problems again.

I remember a service where a woman suddenly showed up at the back and started walking down the middle aisle. She hissed and strutted in such a way that you just knew something was wrong. Allen ignored her and kept on preaching. The lady strutted back out of the auditorium. Just then Allen stopped. He said very calmly and sweetly, "Now, demon, you weren't dismissed. You know you can't leave this place without permission. You had the nerve to interrupt my sermon. You knew what was going to happen when you did that. Get back in here." Well, the lady came right back in as if she were hypnotized, came right up to the front, and was delivered.

The Scriptures talk about "power over demons." Well, A.A. Allen had that. If he gained a reputation for dealing with demons, then it was because his whole purpose was to meet the needs of the people. He looked for the hardest cases. He didn't shrink away, and any doctor can tell you that people with psychiatric problems are often the hardest cases.

Was it a gift?

That's a hard one. The Bible talks about *discerning of spirits* as a gift. It doesn't talk about *deliverance* as a gift. This indicates that all believers have power over demons. The Bible says, "Resist the devil, and he will flee from you" (Jas. 4:7b). But it also tells the story of a deliverance that Jesus performed. When it was over, the disciples asked Him how He did it. They said that they had tried but couldn't exorcise the demon. Jesus explained to them that "...this kind goeth not out but by prayer and fasting" (Mt. 17:21).

I would have to say that the ability to perform an exorcism takes the gift of faith. Allen's faith was a gift, and his experience helped him tremendously. He knew what to expect. Also, he was ready. He knew that there would possibly be demonic activity in each service, and so he would often pray and fast before it began.

There is a funny story about some of the young preachers in training at Allen's Miracle Valley Bible School. One of them was leading the service when it was suddenly interrupted by a demonic manifestation. You have to understand. People came to Miracle Valley from all over the world, and you never knew what their problem would be. Well, this young preacher started commanding the demon to leave, but nothing seemed to be happening. He ordered it out in Jesus' name. He used every formula that he knew, yet the demon-possessed person just sneered back at him with a smirk. Finally, he said, "You better leave now, before Reverend Allen gets out here, because you know you're gonna have to go then, and it won't be pleasant." Well, everybody broke up with laughter.

But the lesson learned was that it wasn't as easy as it looked. That's why most of the other evangelists ducked the whole issue. It may also explain why they criticized A.A. Allen. Maybe they were being a little too defensive. He obviously had power in that area that they didn't have.

But there were stories of people vomiting out frogs. There were charges of fraud.

These deliverance sessions were often accompanied by vomiting. It was really very sickening. And yet even today when there is an exorcism, Catholic or Protestant, it is often accompanied by vomiting. On one occasion, a woman coughed up something that looked like a small frog. She was a pretty wild lady. Now, whether she had swallowed it before in some satanic ritual or if she was just a poor soul seeking attention, I don't know. But something like that did happen. It was only a one-time event. The only explanation Allen could find was the verse of Revelation 16:13: "And I saw three unclean spirits like frogs...."

The point is, the single event was not turned into a doctrine. In fact, nothing like it ever happened again. After A.A. Allen's fight with the denominations began, there were all kinds of charges, but his magazine still exists in the archives. Everything is there for anybody who really wants to know the truth. Vomiting out frogs was not part of the program. Nobody claimed that. Stories were exaggerated. People who were critical wanted to believe the exaggerated stories, and so they spread.

What about the oil? There were stories that oil began to appear on people's hands and foreheads.

It was true. It did happen. I saw people empty Kleenex packages trying to absorb it all. Sometimes it would happen to the whole audience. Skeptics and unbelievers would sit there with scowls on their faces and drops of oil forming on their foreheads. I suppose it could be compared to being slain in the Spirit or to the spirit of joy that accompanies Rodney Howard-Browne's ministry of today. It was just a physical manifestation of the Spirit passing by.

What was the rationale? How was it explained or justified?

In Scripture, oil represents the Holy Spirit. The prophets anointed people with oil. James wrote in the New Testament that when people were sick, "...let him call for the elders of the church; and let them pray over him, anointing him with oil in the name of the Lord: and the prayer of faith shall save the sick, and the Lord shall raise him up; and if he have committed sins, they shall be forgiven him" (Jas. 5:14-15). Allen also used to quote Psalm 133:2 about the precious oil flowing down from Aaron's beard.

It happened one night when people started getting oil on their hands or foreheads before A.A. Allen could touch them. Ironically, I think it was during the Knoxville, Tennessee, crusade, which later became famous because of Allen's fight with the Assemblies of God and because there were the charges that he had been drinking and driving. The manifestation of oil started with a little six-year-old boy named Lavin Burcham. Then it began happening to all kinds of people almost everywhere we went. We have old films of R.W. Shambach sitting on the platform with oil on his hands. I remember a woman in Oakland. She came to all of our West Coast crusades, and the oil just poured off of her. She could hold out her hands, and the oil would just pop out of her pores. It would fill her shoes, and they would squeak when she walked across the platform. It was amazing.

But couldn't it have been psychological? Might it have been some sort of physiological response?

I don't know. But it doesn't make any difference. It amazed and touched the hearts of the people in the audience. Of course, it doesn't translate very well when you explain it to people who weren't there experiencing it for themselves, but then neither does the Rodney Howard-Browne phenomenon. A.A. Allen called it a "wonder." The Bible says that signs and wonders will follow them that believe (see Mk. 16:17). "Have you ever seen a wonder?" Allen would ask. "What is a wonder? A wonder is something that makes people wonder." And then he would point dramatically to the oil flowing from these people. "Well, this is a wonder."

The criticism was that Allen was a big promoter and that he made too big a deal out of it—that this kind of emphasis lacked balance.

It's true. Some said that the whole healing revival lacked balance. For example, there was not the same amount of emphasis on the other gifts of the Spirit as there was on healing. And certainly, in the light of eternity, what difference does a healing make? If we believe the promise of God that we will all live on in some way even beyond this lifetime, what difference does it make if we are crippled, or blind, or deaf in this life? How can we compare a few years of pain with eternity?

The only answer I can give is that the gifts of healing had lain dormant within the Church for years. It took something shocking to jar people loose. And then, when we speak of balance, was the ministry of Jesus balanced? There are healings and exorcisms on every page of His story. He seemed to care how people hurt, even in this brief lifetime.

But we were talking about the oil.

Yes. A.A. Allen was a promoter, and when he believed in something, he was a fighter. The oil phenomenon happened about the time of his split with the Assemblies of God, and when their ministers started attacking it, Allen defended it all the more.

He was a great believer in God confirming the word that you preach. In other words, what you preached should happen. If one preached healing, then it should happen that night. If one preached tithing, then that person should take up an offering. If one preached joy, there should be joy. I have to tell you that when A.A. Allen preached joy it was every bit as powerful as a Rodney Howard-Browne service, but it didn't happen every night. When he preached miracles, miracles happened. Some nights he preached salvation and thousands would be saved. He was one of the greatest soul winners of his generation.

Was there fanaticism? Was there fraud?

I am sure there were some abuses, just as there is in any move of God.

What happened with the Assemblies of God? What was the drunk driving scandal all about?

A.A. Allen and the Assemblies of God were on a collision course even before the drunk driving incident. There were open battles between the healing evangelists and the Assemblies hierarchy. There were hotheads on both sides who wanted to fan the flames and heat up the argument. By this time, Jack Coe had already been disfellowshipped.

A.A. Allen was a target. That's important for understanding what happened in this story. I don't think we'll ever understand all of it. Allen is gone, and he was a very private man. I picked up bits and pieces of it from what his wife Lexie told me over the years, but much of it will remain a mystery.

Basically, he had an alcohol problem as a youth and from time to time he had relapses. Given the facts surrounding his troubled childhood and the daily pressure of the crusades, it is remarkable that he was able to keep going as he did. The relapses were very, very rare. They were so rare, in fact, that his closest team members were not all aware of it, and they would fiercely defend his honor when charges were raised.

The newspapers in Knoxville, Tennessee, had been targeting him and other evangelists for several years. In the case of Allen, it just all came together one night. He was arrested on a DUI charge, driving under the influence of alcohol. The next day, he met with the local Assemblies of God presbyters. They had him now, and they knew it. He had been a big shot. Some may have understandably been a little jealous over his following. Many were upset because their own people were supporting Allen financially. Now, they had him.

Basically, he agreed to go through a period of repentance and rehabilitation, and they agreed to salvage his ministry by handling it all discreetly. According to Allen's wife, Lexie, they looked him in the eye and said, "This is between us. We are ministers, and our job is reconciliation and rehabilitation. We don't judge you; we just want to help you. If you will humble yourself and go through a period of counseling, we will help restore your ministry."

Now, this was not adultery. This did not involve anyone else but Allen. It was, nevertheless, very serious. Pentecostals and Christians from the holiness tradition looked on alcohol as deeply sinful. Allen himself publicly preached strongly against it.

As soon as the private meeting with the Assemblies of God brethren was dismissed, one of the preachers went right to the Knoxville newspapers and gleefully told them the whole story. It was on the wire that evening and went all across the country. Allen was ruined, or so some of them intended.

Up to that point, A.A. Allen had been fully willing to go along with whatever the denomination recommended. He knew that many of them wanted to destroy him and that there were misunderstandings. But he was humiliated by what had happened. I believe he sincerely wanted help. He thought that in spite of the disagreements that these men were brothers in the Lord and that, as brothers, he could trust them to be fair. But the treachery of those ministers left him cold. As far as he was concerned, he had been set up. They had milked him of all the information they could get out of him, yet they had never intended to help him; they wanted only to destroy him. As far as he was concerned, their lie was even worse than his lack of temperance.

Now, that may not be fair. Maybe most of the presbyters were sincere. Maybe only one took it upon himself to betray Allen. But I know this: A.A. Allen was not a drunk. He was a man of God. I was with him almost every day for 10 years and could count maybe 15 times at the most that he relapsed. He was preaching every single night of the year. It was exhausting and grueling. He was not a rich man. He did not live ostentatiously. He ministered to the poorest of the poor, the people whom all the other evangelists shunned. When he died in 1970, his entire estate was listed at only $100,000, and he left every penny of it to the ministry. I can tell you that he left that Knoxville experience believing that the denomination was corrupt. All bets were off. He left the Assemblies of God, and they kicked him out. It was over.

Was he an alcoholic?

I don't know. He may have been. But let me clarify that. He didn't really have a drinking problem. There were very, very few instances where the bottle got the better of him. But, yes, in the clinical sense of the word, he may have been one of the 18 percent or so of the population that had a pre-disposition for alcoholism. In Alcoholics Anonymous they teach you to recognize the fact that you have the problem and to never forget it even when you stop drinking. It can come back, so don't get cocky. Basically they teach, "Once an alcoholic, always an alcoholic."

As I pointed out, his father was an alcoholic. And in his early years, Allen was one as well. He just never seemed to be able to confront the problem. Who could he go to? Who could he trust? He didn't really believe that a secular, non-believing counselor could help. Could he go to a rival evangelist, someone who was basically competing for the same support from their own magazines and radio programs? He had learned pretty early that he couldn't trust his own denomination. They would only exploit any weakness. So, he just dealt with it alone, and in his own way.

What was the reaction?

His detractors had a field day. They called him a hypocrite, a drunk. His friends, including his own evangelistic team, defended him, saying that it wasn't true, which actually made things even worse. There was obviously an official police record of the incident. Members of his team said that it was a "frame-up."

Now, even denominational leaders who had sympathized with him had to abandon him. Finally, he and *The Voice of Healing* parted ways. He was in the wilderness.

But he survived?

He thrived. The crisis forced him to learn how to operate without the churches as a base. He had a good team of godly men led by Kent Rogers and R.W. Shambach. When the revival began to wane in this country, A.A. Allen was still going strong because he had learned how to build a new and more invulnerable base of support.

Which was?

He went directly to the masses, bypassing the churches. After the split with *The Voice of Healing*, he launched his own *Miracle Magazine*, which eventually reached a circulation of two million. He learned how to make radio actually pay big. He became a pioneer in understanding the science of mailing lists, something that my own ministry was able to build on and take even much further. Allen was the only healing evangelist besides Oral Roberts to actually launch a successful television ministry, although his audience never rivaled the size of Roberts'. Allen also turned even more to the masses of poor, to the blacks, to the outcasts of America. He identified with them, he loved them, and they knew it.

The healing revival was pretty famous for breaking the racial barriers. How do you explain it?

Again, I would have to say that the miracles were genuine, and people could sense the Spirit of God. They just couldn't harbor any kind of hatred or bigotry in that atmosphere. Yet you must give some credit to the boldness of the evangelists themselves.

Maria Woodworth-Etter conducted integrated meetings throughout the South and was persecuted by local authorities because of it. Even the newspapers ripped her for this stand. William Branham and Oral Roberts both insisted that their Southern crusades be "open." Jack Coe welcomed blacks to his meetings. But by the late 1950's, A.A. Allen was the favorite of black audiences all across the country. They loved him, and he loved them back.

In Atlanta, Georgia, as late as 1960, we were required to segregate the audiences. To get a permit to use the fairgrounds, you had to agree to post signs reading "White Section" and "Colored Section." But Allen would get the people praising God with very upbeat Gospel Soul music, and the people would soon be dancing back and forth across the line. He purposely integrated the healing line, and by the third night of a crusade, everybody was sitting wherever they wanted.

It was during the Atlanta meeting that Allen discovered Gene Martin. This young black singer had such a voice that it could be heard above the whole congregation. Kent Rogers told A.A. Allen about him, and they agreed to have him sing a solo for the afternoon service. Well, Martin sang, "I Know the Lord Will Make a Way for Me." It was deeply moving to whites and blacks alike. Allen hired him on the spot, and Gene Martin became a fixture at our crusades for the next ten years.

You know, I visited in many black homes during those years, and again and again I would see on the wall pictures of John Kennedy, Martin Luther King, and A.A. Allen. He was loved. If there were weaknesses in his life, they were forgiven.

You picked up right where he left off.

Well, I began ministering when the Civil Rights crisis was at its peak. Allen wanted some of us young members of the team to have some experience, so he sent us out.

I remember an incident in Charleston, South Carolina, in 1963. I had an old tent. It had so many holes that you could look up and see the stars at night. There were about 50 people in the audience that first night. Well, the county required the posting of signs "White Section," "Colored Section." It didn't strike me as the right thing to do. These black folk were my brothers and sisters in the Lord. God had created us both. I was 22 years old and very bold.

The next night, in the middle of the service, two big policemen came down the middle aisle of the tent, right up onto the platform, and arrested me. I was put in handcuffs in front of the whole audience and taken off to jail.

Word spread through the community, and the hearing the next morning was packed with Christians. The judge asked me if I wanted a lawyer. They all knew that I didn't have any money. So I stood up and quoted the verses in the Bible where Jesus says that if they bring you before the magistrates and judges, you should take no thought about what you will say, for in that hour He will give you the words (see Mt. 10:17-20).

"Your Honor," I said, "Jesus is my lawyer. He will defend me."

Well, the audience went crazy. An old black woman stood up in the middle of court and started speaking in tongues. The judge was dumbfounded. Then someone else stood up and interpreted the message, saying, "Touch not My anointed servant. Do him no harm."

The judge pounded his gavel. "Bailiff, clear the courtroom, clear the courtroom. Bailiff, clear the courtroom." But nothing happened, and then the people broke into singing. It was amazing. What could the judge do? Throw everybody in jail? Later the bailiff said that his father had been a Pentecostal preacher, and he wasn't about to touch those people.

Finally, as a face-saving device more than for any other reason, the judge made me agree to close the meetings at 11 p.m. and then dismissed all charges. Well, I walked out into the sunshine, and there was a huge crowd of church people standing on the front steps of the courthouse, cheering me on. That night the tent was packed. I stayed six weeks. The crowds reached 1,500 people. From the offerings, we bought a new tent, a Hammond organ, and a semi-trailer truck to haul everything back. A.A. Allen was pleased. I was learning that there was a definite calling on our ministry to preach to the poor.

Did the news spread?

Oh sure. After that there were controversies wherever I went across the South. In Elberton, Georgia, the Ku Klux Klan showed up in full regalia. They burned crosses in front of our tent. Our night watchman ran off into the night and never came back. But Allen had taught us from example to use controversy to our advantage. Talk bad about us, talk good about us—just don't stop talking about us.

Chapter Six

The Great International Crusades

Clifton Erickson, Lester Sumrall, Tommy Hicks, William Branham, and T.L. Osborn

We have in our archives several old reels of 16 millimeter film. They show scenes from the great Rio de Janeiro crusades of Clifton Erickson, and they are really something to see. We're talking about the *mid*-1950's. Soccer stadiums couldn't hold these crowds. They had to move out into open fields.

Erickson would pray for healing en masse. Then he would call for those who claimed miracles to come to the front. His staffers were there to interview these people and bring the best testimonies to the platform. It was a method that would later be used by Kathryn Kuhlman and Morris Cerullo, and it is quite similar to the approach I am still using in our crusades in the Philippines and across the Pacific rim.

Well, it was electrifying. All the focus was on the very few, absolutely verifiable healings. "What is your name? Where do you live? What is the name of your doctor? What hospital were you in? Is there anyone here who works at that hospital? Can you confirm this?"

Erickson would interview the family members who would be weeping with joy and be completely overcome with emotion. You could just feel the faith rise in the audience. It was remarkably effective. Then the healings would start to happen faster than they could be reported. The local journalists didn't know what to do. Some of them just reported it straight. In some of these Latin American crusades there were headlines with testimonies of the healings. For several years, when Erickson went to Rio de Janeiro or Sao Paulo, those huge cities almost shut down.

My father and mother were guests of the Erickson crusade team during some of those years. They talked about it long after-ward. And then they were brought along on the later Cerullo crusades.

Roy Wead [Doug Wead's father] was courted by all those guys be-cause of his position as a leader in the Assemblies of God. They knew that he was pretty tolerant and open to the healing ministry, so they looked to him for legitimacy.

You probably heard about Erickson's big crusade in Manila. It also captured headlines, and it really helped build a huge church there, which Lester Sumrall pastored and led.

I remember reading about an exorcism in Manila. It was a very sensational case, even capturing the headlines for a few days.

It happened in 1953 at the height of the revival. The name of the girl was Clarita Villaneuva, and yes, it was very much a celebrated inci-dent, receiving worldwide notoriety. Clarita was a 17-year-old native girl from the countryside who had been picked up off the streets of Manila by the police, charged with vagrancy, and thrown into the Bilibid prison. Right away the newspapers and radio started reporting strange things happening.

The girl claimed that she was being attacked in her cell by two "dev-ils." When the attacks would take place, she would scream with agony and sometimes foam at the mouth. These incidents could last for hours, and then she would lose consciousness. The police and doctors were afraid that she would hurt herself, so they had gone into the cell during one of these bouts of hysteria and physically restrained her and held her. Then her body broke out with bite marks all over it.

As you can imagine, the newspapers and radio had a field day: "Girl bitten by devils." Manila was captivated by the story. The attacks seemed to take place at night. So, every night, the Bilibid prison was crowded with observers—psychiatrists, psychologists, medical doctors of every kind, professors, police specialists, and every journalist who could get credentials. Sometimes Clarita would talk sensibly and normally, answering any questions that were asked of her. But when the attacks began, she was uncontrollable.

And the claim of bite marks was ongoing? It happened more than once?

Oh, yes, that was what was driving the story. She was under 24-hour surveillance to make sure that she wasn't somehow biting herself, although they had found the marks in places where she couldn't possibly have bitten herself. On one occasion, police and doctors entered the cell to restrain her. Afterward, they claimed that they had even found bite marks on her wrists where they had restrained her. All sorts of stories started spreading. They had supposedly found hairs in the cell that weren't Clarita's or that of the attendant police and doctors.

Well, at the time, an American missionary by the name of Lester Sumrall was in Manila. He was in the process of establishing a new congregation in the city and had been very successful with one exception: he couldn't find a place to put everybody. He had outgrown the auditoriums that he had rented, and he was running into difficulty getting a building permit to do something on his own. Like the rest of the city, he sat by his radio one night listening to a report from inside the Bilibid prison. According to Sumrall, the screams of the girl and her pleas for help sent chills down your spine. The girl was obviously in terror, and to Sumrall, she was not sick, she was demon possessed.

Now, Lester Sumrall was not the typical healing evangelist. He was something of a missionary statesman. He was a personal friend of the famous archaeologist Howard Carter, the man who had discovered King Tut's tomb in Egypt. Sumrall had been a best-selling religious author, and for years he had pastored one of the largest Pentecostal churches in the United States. At a time when Pentecostals were usually not very educated and were quite poor, Sumrall came off as very erudite and savvy. He was something of a Lowell Thomas, a traveling celebrity-adventurer. He would have been perfectly in place at a society dinner, and more than likely, would have been the most popular guest. Anyway, the next day he walked into the mayor's office and asked for permission to pray for the girl. The mayor said, "Okay." Sumrall went in and prayed for the girl. She was delivered and the rest is history.

The exorcism took place in front of all those professional witnesses?

Oh, yes. The police and doctors weren't about to let that girl out of their sight. At first, Sumrall asked to be alone with the girl—perhaps he was afraid that he would be inhibited by the outsiders and non-believers—but they wouldn't allow it. This was very much a public thing. Everybody wanted in on it, which turned out to be a great thing because after the exorcism, when the girl was perfectly normal, Sumrall became an instant celebrity. It was all over the front pages. The mayor asked Sumrall what he could do for him. Sumrall said that he needed a building permit, and so a great church, Bethel Temple, Manila, started going up.

Tell me about the exorcism. What happened?

After Sumrall got permission from the mayor, the doors to Bilibid prison were open to him. He could go in whenever he wanted. But, very wisely, he went home, where he spent the next day and night in prayer and fasting.

When Sumrall met Clarita the next morning, the demons manifested themselves immediately. He spent from 9:00 in the morning till 12:00 noon, wrestling and praying over the girl. Everyone was watching, and they were astonished. He would adjure the demons to leave in the name of Jesus. They would shout back through the girl, cursing him and saying that they weren't leaving.

When the demons overwhelmed Clarita, she could speak in perfect English to Sumrall. She would curse him violently and shout and rave. She said that God was the one who was evil. She cursed the blood of Jesus. Many of the observers needed interpreters to understand what she was saying because they themselves could not understand English. Where had this poor, vagrant girl from the countryside learned it? And where had she learned such complex theological terms and concepts? Well, Sumrall believed that the knowledge and the words she was using were coming through the power of the demons. They were the ones who were talking. When she calmed down and the demons left her alone, she would return to normal for a few hours. Then Sumrall would need an interpreter, for she could only speak Tagalog.

The next day, Sumrall was back, and the battle continued. But this time, Sumrall finally sensed that the demons were about to go. He ordered everyone around him onto their knees. He told them that the demons were going to come out and that they should be reverent and respectful or he could not assume responsibility for them. The demons could very well go into one of them. Well, the people were all on their knees in a flash—journalists, professors, hardened policemen—everybody. Then, Sumrall made the police and doctors promise that there would be no drugs or medication after her deliverance. He wanted the girl to be lucid so that she could explain what had happened to her.

This time, after a few minutes of prayer, Clarita broke into a peaceful smile. She began to weep softly, announcing to the whole group in her Tagalog language that it was over; she had felt the demons go. "There is no doubt," she said. "It's over."

A prisoner in another nearby cell who had been mocking at the whole scene, laughing loudly as Sumrall prayed, suddenly gave out a bloodcurdling cry. For a moment there was some panic. This second woman now claimed that she had felt one of the demons pass by her and that she had been bitten. A few minutes before, she had been mocking. Now she was begging for prayer. So Sumrall prayed for her.

Well, it had been an astonishing experience. Dr. Lars of the Bilibid prison was flabbergasted. When it was finished, Sumrall called the mayor's office and declared, "The devil is dead!" Of course, some of the observers were still not so sure. They kept the girl under surveillance for days, but nothing more happened. It was over. The newspapers that had made a big deal out of it before the exorcism now had no choice but to play it straight. Clarita had been delivered. The whole story is still there in the archives.

Later that year, right on the heels of this publicity, Lester Sumrall helped bring Clifton Erickson to town. With Erickson came those mighty miracles of healings. Crowds swelled into the hundreds of thousands. In four weeks, almost a quarter of a million people converted to Christianity. So a great church was born, and from it many other churches came.

So, there were many remarkable stories from these international crusades. In some cases, they were just as powerful as the crusades under William Branham or Smith Wigglesworth. The late Lester Sumrall also ran a small Christian television network and was a popular speaker. Clifton Erickson, who is now deceased, was a very humble man and had once been a truck driver. He had never been good at promoting himself, and as a result, he built no ongoing organization. When the mammoth crusades were finally over, so was Erickson's large, international ministry.

By the early 1960's, Morris Cerullo had picked up where Clifton Erickson had left off in South America. Cerullo had huge crusades all over the Third World. But he was very careful to maintain a financial base in the United States, which helped sustain his ministry afterward. Today, Cerullo is still holding successful union meetings in the United Kingdom.

Tommy Hicks' big crusades in Argentina got lots of attention.

Hicks got started in Latin America even before the Clifton Erickson meetings. One of the most famous crusades was held in Buenos Aires, Argentina. Some estimates put a single night attendance at 400,000. Hicks was invited to the presidential palace and was photographed with President Juan Peron.

Hicks then took a tour behind the Iron Curtain. He couldn't actually hold meetings there, of course, but he came back with some remarkable stories and became the darling of the Full Gospel Businessmen's speaking circuit.

Were these international crusades self-supporting?

Yes and no. The successful crusades paid for themselves, but the ministries had to survive in between crusades, and most of them refused to take money from the Christians in these countries, some of which were very poor. So they ended up competing for those very scarce dollars back in America, where thousands of evangelists were now feeling the pinch. Yet they generally competed successfully. They had more to show for the dollar. In essence, an evangelist could say, "Look how many souls your dollar can win in Africa or South America."

Almost all of them began going abroad. It became a rite of passage. It was almost as if you couldn't really claim to have a valid American ministry unless you could talk about your crusades in other countries.

You have to remember that from the very beginning of the revival, there had been an international emphasis. We talked about John Dowie's tours around the world back in the nineteenth century. Such international travel was extremely rare and financially prohibitive at the time. Charles Price held meetings all across Europe and the Middle East.

Keep in mind that the healing movement emphasized the New Testament and especially the Great Commission, where Jesus said to go into all the world and preach the gospel and heal the sick. So you can see that healing and worldwide ministry have a special scriptural link. You can't become the champion of one without becoming the champion of the other.

William Branham had some remarkable crusades in Europe and Africa. Oral Roberts spoke to large auditorium audiences in major cities all over the world and held some large open-air African crusades. A.A. Allen went to Ghana, South America, and the Philippines. Actually, Allen founded a Bible school that trained hundreds of native missionaries and preachers. This is the work I picked up when I inherited the Allen ministry. Over the past few years my team and I have built more than 300 churches in the Philippines. Really, this is part of Allen's legacy. He may not have actually built the churches, but he built the Bible school, and that helped start it all.

What did they think of William Branham in some of these other countries? How did foreign journalists react, for example?

Branham's gift was so outstanding that he did well wherever he went, even in Europe where his limited education could have been a real liability. In fact, one of Branham's more famous visions came true in Finland. He had told it all over the United States, and Gordon Lindsay, aware of the importance of verification, had made sure that many of these visions were notarized. When it came true in Finland, the local journalists were dumbfounded.

In South Africa there were massive crowds and a long succession of healings that defied any natural explanation. A headline in *The Durban Sunday Tribune* said, "'Miracle' Sets Boy Walking." *The Natal Mercury* declared, "Bedridden Woman Walks At Evangelist's Command." In fact, the best accounts of Branham's meetings were in the national press, who aggressively followed up on the apparent healings by interviewing doctors, relatives, employers, and neighbors.

Branham would turn and point at someone in the audience, "You, madam, are suffering from arthritis. You have not been able to raise your hand above your head in years. God healed you ten minutes ago. Raise your hand, now." Well, the journalists were all over her like a disease: *Did she really have arthritis? Was it true that she hadn't been able to raise her hand above her head? Could she do it now? What was her name? Where did she live? Had she ever seen the evangelist before? How did she think the evangelist knew she had arthritis? Had she written it down anywhere or told anyone nearby who could have tipped him off? Had she felt anything unusual ten minutes before? What was the name of her doctor?*

The press in South Africa, with the thoroughness and skepticism that good journalists must have, did more for the crusades than Gordon

Lindsay himself ever could have done. Eventually, thousands of miracles were documented. The nation of South Africa was beside itself.

Incidentally, it was a very short trip, but its impact was felt for years, even generations.

How?

Well, take Durban, for example. He was only there five days. They had promoted his coming for months. There were posters everywhere, and Pentecostal churches were united. He had already been in South Africa for several days, and stories of his meetings elsewhere were electric. The local journalists were salivating to get their shot at him. When it opened they had the largest, single crowd for a religious service ever. Four thousand people packed into MacKenzie Hall.

Now, in a Billy Graham crusade or a crusade with any other evangelist, that's what you get; if you start with 4,000, you get an audience of 4,000 the next night too. Whatever your promotion and organization has been able to turn out that first night becomes your basic attendance for the crusade.

Branham's crusades were different. No matter how many stories the people had heard, they were never ready for what happened in those meetings. The sweetness of the presence of God was almost tangible. Branham was like an Old Testament prophet, a seer. People were astonished when it happened right in their own city. The next night in Durban the crowd doubled. Four thousand people stood in the rain outside MacKenzie Hall, listening on loudspeakers.

Night after night, the audience would double or triple. The first night a single journalist or two would come. The next day, it would be the talk of the newsroom. The next night, the whole newsroom would show up. The following night, the editors would be there. Eventually, the publisher and his family would be there, and his sick aunt would be flying in on a private plane from Johannesburg. Even the publisher's maid, houseboy, and the houseboy's neighbor who had cancer would show up. (I'm speaking figuratively now.) But the same thing would happen in hospitals and office buildings. In Durban, for example, by the last night, the city had helped Branham find a racetrack that was available. Tens of thousands showed up, filling the grandstands and the infield, with tens of thousands more standing outside.

What these people saw and experienced in a few short days was enough to last a lifetime. The Pentecostal churches bulged with new members, but there was not room for them all, and most would not have been able to make the social and cultural adjustment anyway. But they went back to their traditional Christian church haunted and changed by what they had seen.

You have talked about it affecting generations?

Well, the people, in their own way, would pass on their thoughts to their children. Thinking back to what they had seen and heard, they might say that, yes, in some circumstances, they believed that God did heal the sick. When the charismatic renewal hit South Africa, thousands of Catholics and Anglicans were swept up into it, and the old-timers among them often spoke back to the Branham visit. So, the crusade was only five days long, but it had its impact.

And yet, a Tommy Hicks crusade brought in 400,000 in a single night?

Well, Branham didn't really go to one of the developing nations. During his time in South Africa, he did speak to large black crowds in the townships. But anyone who has traveled to South Africa knows that it is not a so-called "Third World country." He also visited the United Kingdom, Switzerland, and Scandinavia. No one really knows what would have happened if Branham had gone to Brazil or the Philippines.

Branham also didn't have the organization and advance work behind him that Oral Roberts, Tommy Hicks, and the others had. The locals had to organize the meeting pretty much on their own.

Were there similar, lasting results from these mass meetings of Oral Roberts, Tommy Hicks, and Clifton Erickson?

The one you are forgetting was T.L. Osborn, who had the greatest international ministry of all. To answer your question, yes, there were spectacular results, and they were lasting. By any measure, the legacy of Osborn and Erickson and others is huge. In many Latin American countries today, the Pentecostals are the largest religious bloc.

Incidentally, it is hard to measure that strength. Catholics, of course, are older and have more political and social clout, but when you actually count Catholic population you count the number of those baptized Catholic, which includes infants, children, and people who are no longer even attending Mass. Pentecostals don't practice infant baptism, and in a reaction to the Catholic emphasis on Church membership, they don't emphasize that as well. There are huge Pentecostal churches with

10,000 in attendance and only 300 official members, so when you see a count, it generally doesn't reflect the real strength of the group. That has been a remarkable discovery for modern Latin American politicians and public relations firms. Recently, the Pentecostals have helped elect several new presidents in Central and Latin America, including the president of Peru.

Well, Osborn and the other leaders of mass evangelism had their role to play in that vast Pentecostal revival in those regions.

When one thinks of Osborn, one thinks of his crusade in Java.

It was historic, and yet in terms of sheer numbers, it was actually typical of an Osborn campaign—just another day at the office. With the possible exception of the Tommy Hicks crusade in Argentina, these Osborn crusades were the largest that had ever been conducted. And there was a big difference. It had happened once for Tommy Hicks, and with Osborn, it kept happening over and over again.

You have no idea how much work is involved in a crusade like that. As the crowd swells, the organizers have to scramble to find another location. People will spend two or three years planning a mass crusade like that, and all of a sudden they have to start over again, with 24 hours to advertise the new location, have a public address system that will work, and have all the government permits. It is a mess, and it is risky. You have to have a lot of flexibility. You must be willing to delegate, and you must accept the fact that there will be many mistakes. But the end results are truly astounding. The city, even the nation, was often shaken by a T.L. Osborn campaign.

But they made a movie about Java.

Osborn produced several missionary films, and they were popular. By that time the Assemblies of God and other official denominations were feuding with the *Voice of Healing* evangelists. Most of them were blacklisted from the churches. But they couldn't keep T.L. Osborn films from proliferating and circulating. They were everywhere. There was nothing else like them available. They were educational, colorful, and they offered vignettes of the healing revival as it spread around the world.

The event that caused such a stir in Java was the "Jesus in the clouds." Thousands of people claimed that a cloud formation above the crusade had formed into a perfect picture of Jesus. Later, someone sent in a photograph, and sure enough, there it was. It was just the cloud formation, of course, but it was a very perfect picture.

There was a big controversy about it. Some people were critical, saying that it was gimmick, but Osborn hadn't invented it. Thousands of people personally attested to it. What can you do?

You can ignore it. If it is controversial, why make a big deal?

Well, you always have that choice, but then you are like the religious leaders in the time of Jesus who attributed His miracles to anything and everything but Him. Finally, they decided that His miracles were the work of the devil. They just couldn't accept the truth in front of them. What if this was a beautiful sign that God had given these people? How arrogant it would be to ignore it. Our faith is supposed to be simple and childlike.

And yet, it smacks of gimmickry. Why hold yourself up to such criticism? Anyway, what is the scriptural basis for such a claim?

The Bible says that signs and wonders will follow them that believe. We make room for the nine gifts of the Holy Spirit, but there will also be "signs and wonders."

With such huge crowds, there must have been some remarkable testimonies.

Yes, and vice versa. By that I mean that there were first the remarkable testimonies, and then there were the huge crowds. Yes, there were thousands. Again, in terms of sheer numbers, T.L. Osborn may have seen more healings that any other person who has ever lived. And Osborn documented these miracles better than any of his contemporaries did. Even today, you can go into the archives and find the stories and follow up to see what happened years later.

One of my favorite stories happened in his great Puerto Rican campaign. The story involved an old war veteran named Juan Santos. This man was a very proud person, but a World War II bullet to the spine had reduced him to the state of a grotesque cripple. Santos had no feeling below his waist. He was a chronic paraplegic.

Puerto Rico was very poor. The government could not provide much medical assistance. Santos had to be dressed and carried to the toilet by his wife and family. He hated his existence and had often tried to commit suicide. One such attempt had damaged his larynx, so in addition to everything else, his speech became slurred. While the rest of the family ate at the table, he ate like a dog out of a box of food on the floor.

There were no electric wheelchairs then, and he wouldn't have gotten one anyway; they were much too poor. So, Juan Santos moved around the ground with the aid of a strong stick and a carefully shaped block of wood. His legs were lifeless and drawn up under his body like an insect. After 16 years of nonuse, they had withered away to skin and bone.

When I say grotesque, well, you have to imagine this creature, slithering along the sidewalks and gutters. His right arm was useless and drawn in like a chicken wing. His left arm shook with a palsy, and when he spoke, he slobbered and sounded like an idiot. But inside this creature was a dignified, bright, well-read person who was suffering terribly. He grew angry about life, growing to hate the people around him.

When news of the Osborn crusade was passed on to his family, he had no interest. But if Juan Santos wouldn't come to the crusade, then the crusade would come to him. After outgrowing the first location, the Osborn meeting moved across town. In the evening, Santos could hear the public address system, and he began listening to the sermons.

His family imagined that they had spotted a glimmer of hope in him and encouraged him to go. But then, the newspapers reported that 10,000 people had been turned away the previous night. What were the odds that the evangelist would pray for him? What was the use?

And then one night Osborn preached on the paralytic who, because of the crowds, was lowered down into the room for Jesus to heal. The old man wept. Within a few days, Osborn had outgrown the new location and was moving on to a huge baseball stadium seating 50,000. Santos surprised his family by announcing that he wanted to go and that, furthermore, he was going to be healed.

His family members did everything they could to soften the blow and prepare the man for what they knew would be his bitter disappointment. His wife wouldn't go with him; she couldn't stand to see him humiliated and defeated any further.

"I will walk home tonight," Santos declared. His wife feared that he was now a totally broken man. He had even lost his anger, which was probably the only thing that had kept him going.

The night of his healing, Santos was carried into the stadium infield by his sons-in-law. To get through the crowd, they often had to hoist him over the heads and pass him forward like a beach ball. The old man was embarrassed and thankful to finally find a spot near a loudspeaker box to curl up in. His daughters left him with one of his sons-in-law, with plans to come back down from the grandstands to get him later.

Next to Santos was a large Puerto Rican woman who had been born blind. She was also a paralytic, and for some reason she used Santos' body as if it were a sack of potatoes to lean against.

When the sermon had finished, Santos responded to the altar call. He couldn't come forward, but he went through all the prayers from right where he was. Then Osborn led a prayer for the sick. The blind lady next to him screamed out loud, "I can see, I can see."

Santos could feel a chill go down his spine. His son-in-law said, "Look, Dad, your legs are moving. Get up, get up."

The blind lady, who could now see the crippled body lying next to her, tried to help and suddenly found that she had use of her paralyzed arm, which started another round of screaming.

Well, for the first time in 16 years, Juan Santos stood to his feet. When his daughter came down to get him, she wondered where he had gone. She stood there for a moment talking with her husband when she suddenly realized that her father was standing there next to her, towering above her, quietly weeping and praising God. She fell over in a dead faint.

The family just stood there, crying, weeping with joy, and hugging each other. Someone laughed that they had carried Dad in and would now have to carry Sis out.

That night they arrived home late. Just as he had promised, Santos walked into the house. His wife was sleeping. He decided to surprise her in the morning.

She rose early, noticed nothing different, and started working on breakfast in the kitchen. Juan Santos awakened with a smile. Yes, his legs still worked. It had not been a dream. He quietly dressed himself and walked into the kitchen. His wife saw the tall man standing before her, imagined him to be an intruder, and let out a bloodcurdling scream.

"It's me," Juan Santos laughed. "It's only me. I told you I would walk home last night, and I did." Like her daughter, she too fell over in a dead faint.

What made the story so effective was all the government medical records. He was a veteran and had to make regular visits to the doctors. There were mountains of paperwork. Everything was so easily documented. Actually, being blind since birth is much more of a miracle, but the Santos story really took on a life of its own.

There were, honestly, thousands of such stories in the Osborn meetings. T.L. Osborn was, in many respects, the greatest of all the healing evangelists. He had Oral Roberts organizational talents and financial acumen. He had Branham's mysticism, and he was by far the best theologian and writer of the bunch, though not as prolific as Gordon Lindsay. Even to this day, no one has written anything better about healing.

And as you mentioned, he has the legacy of all those churches.

Which is the most remarkable part of it all. Actually, in the beginning, T.L. Osborn worked closely with the Pentecostal denominations in each country. He had local Assemblies of God, Foursquare, Church of God, and Pentecostal Holiness missionaries involved. He gave away thousands of dollars to local projects. He built churches and schools. Osborn had enemies and those who were jealous, but they were far outnumbered by his friends.

The whole idea of native evangelism or indigenous missions has been the secret to the worldwide growth of the Assemblies of God and much of that originated with these evangelists.

That's true. That was also part of the very important legacy of Osborn. Right from the beginning, he was holding mammoth crusades across the world. And right from the beginning he trained local evangelists and pastors to take over. When the revival started to taper off in the United States, Osborn was getting even stronger overseas.

That's why I question those historians who suggest that the revival ended in 1953. Don't people of black, brown, or yellow skin count? If one is measuring the revival in numbers of people healed and converted, then it reached its peak in the late 1950's and early 60's. And T.L. Osborn's ministry would be, by far, the most powerful and the most lasting of all the healing evangelists.

The point you make about the Great Commission is well taken. I can understand how the revival would go international. Why did it leave the Untied States? Why didn't it spread to other places and also continue in North America?

Those of us who are a part of what happened would say that it was God's timing. He had something else brewing. Right on the heels of the healing revival came the charismatic renewal in the traditional Christian churches. First, there was the renewal among the Episcopalians—bishops praying for the sick and speaking in tongues. Then it spread to the

Presbyterians. Eventually, there was the renewal at Notre Dame, when it began to spread among Catholics. Today, by most estimates, there are as many Catholic Pentecostals as there are so-called classical Pentecostals in the world.

When Jesus explained to the disciples that He was going to have to leave them, they complained about it. And Jesus said, "You don't know what you are saying. If I don't leave, the Holy Spirit, the Comforter, won't come" (see Jn. 16:7). Well, if the healing revival had droned on in the United States, it is not likely that the great charismatic renewal would have occurred. They involved different cultures, different worlds. The Catholics would never have embraced the peculiar Pentecostal music, the demonstrative worship, and the preaching style, much of which had been borrowed from southern black culture.

What changed when the revival went international? What happened differently?

For one thing, there were no healing lines or tents or ramps. Instead, more and more evangelists prayed for the sick en masse. The formula just worked better.

You could pray for more people. It also avoided charges of "practicing medicine without a license," a charge that was sometimes invoked by people in government who wanted to shut a revival meeting down. Usually, it was a Christian who didn't like the theology of healing.

Then, overseas, the meetings were usually held in a soccer stadium or often in a large open field. They would plaster the city with posters and advertising. The crowds were almost always bigger than in the States.

And it's still going on?

Yes. In 1986, when I held my own crusade in Manila, the local newspapers called it the largest crusade in Philippine history. At one service, the crowd was estimated at 500,000. Later, Billy Graham held what was reported to be an even bigger crusade, and the Pope's visit in 1990 drew a bigger audience yet. But I have experienced the same phenomenon in El Salvador, Guatemala, Brazil, and various African nations. I still go to the Philippines every year.

Reinhard Bonnke is drawing such crowds. Benny Hinn's recent crusades have reportedly drawn more than 300,000 in several African countries, and his ministry is only beginning.

And yet, from the standpoint of religious history, most scholars say that it is over.

And they are right in one sense. The great revival with thousands of evangelists crisscrossing the world is gone. But preceding this great move of God, there were always those single few who carefully carried and embodied these doctrines. There has always been a Lourdes, a place where one can go to find a "point of contact" to touch God for a personal miracle. There are many today who believe that Reinhard Bonnke, Benny Hinn, and others will lead another wave of the anointing that swept the world in the late 1940's and 50's. When it happens, I expect to be a part of it.

Chapter Seven

The Revival in Controversy and Scandal

Marjoe Gortner, Leroy Jenkins, Velmer Gardner, and A.A. Allen

I guess Sinclair Lewis best captured the secular image of the traveling evangelist in the novel, *Elmer Gantry*. Is there any truth to the image? Were there corrupt people on that trail? People such as con men?

There were probably some. But I have to admit that, having met thousands of evangelists and hearing them talk backstage, I never met an Elmer Gantry. I heard about them. They probably existed, although they would be in very, very small company. It would be nothing like the Hollywood portrayals.

For example, some would say that Marjoe Gortner admitted to being essentially a con man. One of my associates has told me of men who got into the ministry just to make money. I've never seen it, and I've seen a lot. In fact, I would say that it would be a pretty difficult thing to do. Why do I say that? Well, if a person is setting out to do something dishonest, why take such a difficult route?

I would expect that even with Marjoe Gortner, there was some ambivalence. I would imagine that his attitude evolved. Probably even today he has doubts about it all. An experience like his would almost have to be second generation.

What do you mean?

Well, it would take a lifetime to learn how to fake it. Very skilled method actors try to portray evangelists on television and in motion pictures and fail at it. Churchgoers find the portrayals absurd. Faking the sincerity and anointing of the Holy Spirit is not easily done. Audiences can tell when there is anointing and when there is not. They will forgive it occasionally. They may even blame it on themselves and their own mood. But if it went on night after night, an evangelist would not last very long. A fake would only attract the most gullible audiences, and even then, not very large audiences.

There was Robert Duvall in *The Apostle*.

Yes, and it was a marvelous, realistic portrayal of a very sincere Pentecostal preacher who lost his cool and killed a man. In fact, it was a very accurate portrayal of a preacher going through the motions. But there was no anointing. No one listening to his sermons in the theaters wept or reported healings. If Robert Duvall took his show on the road, he would attract many lovers of the theater and drama. They would all be mesmerized by his ability to capture the cultural tics and rhythm of a very specific American sub-culture, but he couldn't make it as a minister with just that rhetoric.

That's why I say it would take, at least, a member of a second generation to fake a whole ministry. And it would take a deeply sick person to do it. Gornter grew up in all of this. His parents were evangelists. He was put up there on stage as a little boy preacher. He was essentially trained to do and say the things that people do and say when there is revival. His parents, who originally got him started, were probably very sincere. There had to be the *reality* in order to get the fake. They didn't set out to take advantage of people.

Gortner was just a child when this was going on, so his cynicism was deeply rooted and his experience was a real aberration. And yet, when he grew up, the ministry was all he knew. He couldn't make the transition to anything else. His documentary movie, which was an exposé of the life of an evangelist, was his only chance. He had learned from years on the road how to give an audience what they wanted, how to push the right buttons. So he turned and he gave his secular audience the Elmer Gantry they had always believed in. In that sense, he may have gone from conning the audiences in his religious services to conning his audiences in the secular theaters. That was what people wanted to believe, and he gave it to them. He played to the fictional stereotype of a "hit-and-run," phony preacher. People bought it.

Yet there was Daddy Grace and Father Divine?

They weren't Christian ministers. They can't be compared to the healing evangelists. They were both independent spiritual leaders in the black community with huge cult followings. Father Divine, who came to prominence during the Great Depression, claimed to be God. Essentially, these men offered their followers hope, a way out of poverty. Most of them ran soup kitchens and shelters and did many wonderful Christian works, but they did not teach biblical Christianity.

What about Rev. Ike?

He studied some of the healing evangelists, such as Oral Roberts, Kathryn Kuhlman, and A.A. Allen. I can remember him sitting in Allen's meetings taking notes. But he evolved more into science of the mind doctrine and was not really part of the healing revival. He probably helped give hope to a lot of people by inspiring them to believe in themselves.

But some of the so-called cult leaders evolved out of Christian culture—Jim Jones, for example.

Jim Jones evolved from a Christian culture, yes. But don't suggest that his end result had any connection to that beginning. His story is very, very unique. At the end, Jones ran a Marxist cult, not a Christian cult.

In San Francisco you couldn't just walk in off the street into his services. You had to wait in a long line, and in that line posing as others waiting to get in, were people from the Temple, who would engage you in conversation to see if there were any "reactionary" tendencies. When you got to the front of the line, you were given a little test. If you passed, you were given a copy of *Introduction to Socialism*, which you had to take home and study. Even then, if you passed a second, more comprehensive test and you were finally admitted to your first meeting, you were surrounded by "watchers" who filed reports on how you reacted to the various things that were said and done.

Often, while you sat in the four-hour meeting, someone would visit your home or apartment to look around and come back and slip notes to "father" Jones. So while you still sat there, he could effect a clairvoyant gift or vision and launch into a description of your dining room wall. He would then claim that he had a warning for you or special advice.

This was a real cult. Jones belonged to the Disciples of Christ Church denomination, but only because they allowed each congregation complete autonomy. When other responsible ministers in the denomination criticized what was going on, Jones invoked that sacred issue of "congregational sovereignty," and they would back off. Several times he had Attorney General Freitas visit the congregation in San Francisco. He would then have the people go through the motions of a regular church service. They would pass out Christian hymnals and sing. But when Freitas left, they would take down the pictures of Jesus and put the pictures of Marx back up. Everyone would laugh, and Jones would lead them in various profane chants.

And yet, at one time, Jones was an Assemblies of God minister.

He was for a brief time. As a young man Jones had a reputation for being very ambitious. He had to have the biggest church and the biggest ministry, and he had to have it now. It was all now. He may have had a real conversion experience, but if so, it was quickly corrupted.

The healing revival was at its peak in the mid-1950's, when Jones started getting some attention. He started having Sunday afternoon meetings at the Laurel Street Tabernacle in Indianapolis. Jones had people sign a register when they came into the service, and then he sent a close associate out to nearby addresses to peek in the windows and help give him information so he could sound like William Branham. It impressed some, but others could sense that something was wrong.

Jones and the Assemblies of God eventually parted ways. He went on to lead a great black congregation in Indianapolis and to become a local leader in the "Integration movement," the long-forgotten prelude to the Civil Rights movement. His church developed into a personality cult. Eventually, he moved them all to Redwood, California, then San Francisco, and finally to Guyana were 800 of them died together in a mass suicide.

What about other examples of error or those charged with moral problems?

Through the years the news media have always been quick to spotlight any accusation of fraudulent practices or the moral indiscretions of evangelists. And a couple of their targets have been fairly well known. But let me say this in answer to your question: I believe that we need to be very careful how we talk about and react to other ministers and ministries. Perhaps this attitude comes from my work with A.A. Allen. He would never say an unkind or derogatory word about other preachers.

Unfortunately, there are some people who gloat over the troubles and misfortunes of preachers, especially evangelists. They relish each and every rumor and pass them on with some sort of smug satisfaction. To me, this kind of attitude smacks of arrogance and self-righteousness—as though they would never be guilty of making mistakes or failing. This is the worst form of pride; it's one of the sins that God especially hates. In fact, the sin of pride is far worse in God's sight than some of the things that the most vilified preacher might be guilty of.

For the most part, I feel that evangelists have been unfairly maligned. You need to remember that at the peak of the healing revival, there were thousands of preachers conducting tent and auditorium crusades all over the world. Most of these men were honest, hard-working, and dedicated to their ministries. So, I don't think that we can honestly single out evangelists as the weakest and most likely to fail and disappoint. I'm not trying to gloss over any improprieties that may have occurred, but incidents of fraud or moral corruption were very, very rare.

The problems of evangelists are not any different than the problems of pastors. As a matter of fact, if you could compare a sampling of 200 healing evangelists with a random group of 200 pastors, I doubt there would be any difference at all in the percentage of public failure or embarrassment. You read and hear more about the evangelists because they usually have a higher public profile. Therefore, it's much bigger news when they make a mistake. But the percentages would be about the same.

Frankly, I think the percentage of failure might even be lower for evangelists. They are aware of their high profile and visibility. They know the propensity of the media and skeptics to pounce on even the slightest appearance of indiscretion. So they become very conscious of the need to walk carefully, to protect their public image, knowing that the publicity accompanying the accusation or allegation of a moral failure could destroy their ministry and life's work. For the evangelists I have known, this would be too great a price to pay.

If you think about it, you realize that evangelists, preachers, and pastors are all mere mortals, and like all human beings, they are endowed with the proclivity to failure. No one who is still alive and breathing is exempt from this very natural tendency. But let's talk about failure for a minute and about God's amazing ability to forgive and restore. Think about David's shameful behavior with Bathsheba. He saw her, lusted after her, devised a legal but sinister way to get rid of her soldier husband, and had a child born through this illicit relationship. After all this, God referred to David as a man after His own heart. Also, out of this bloodline came the birth of Jesus, the Savior of the world. So, how do you measure the grace of God? Or the depths of His love—even for people who make miserable mistakes?

The downfall and destruction of a fellow minister is a terrible tragedy. It's nothing to laugh about or take satisfaction in. I try to put myself in his place, and I think about how Jesus would react to the news of a fallen preacher. Everything I read about the life of Jesus in the Scriptures, He was always forgiving, healing, restoring, and lifting. We are all human, and thereby capable of making mistakes. We need to remember that we are not special in the eyes of God because we are "good." We're only special because of His unconditional love and grace. There is always the possibility that "but for the grace of God, there go I."

One of the most frequent accusations of skeptics is the abuse of money by evangelists. Were some of them in it strictly to make money?

There might have been, but none of them were whom I worked with. Think about it. If the object was to make money, why would they choose this, of all things, to be the means? Contrary to public perception, very few evangelists made any money. They lived on the road. They were always one step away from bankruptcy. When A.A. Allen died, his net worth was $100,000, and his organization was millions of dollars in debt. If you compared top evangelists to the top levels of any other profession or discipline, none of them were rich by any comparative, secular standard.

Was there corruption? We talked earlier about audience manipulation. How far did that go? Was there something in between outright fraud and an authentic manifestation of God's power?

The kind of corruption I saw was the kind that came to very sincere, honest men, who found themselves under great financial pressure. They sometimes resorted to temporary, emergency measures. They took very small steps, none of which may have even been wrong in themselves, but at some point they crossed a line and woke up to find themselves on the other side, not even sure how they got there.

Give me an example?

There is a lot of pressure out there. The audience is coming to see God do something miraculous. And, of course, as the evangelist, you know that you can't do anything. It has to be God. So you tend to rely more and more on a formula that has worked in the past. We talked about this earlier. If a certain song moved an audience in Cincinnati, well, maybe it will move the audience in Pittsburgh. It's fair enough reasoning—nothing wrong with that.

Then a certain prophecy that was moving to an audience in one town is repeated in another. There's nothing wrong with that. If this is a prophecy from God, then the whole country needs to hear it. Then some began to find that certain healings were easier than others or that some types of problems are so obviously psychological that in the highly charged atmosphere of the revival the symptoms could be temporarily neutralized.

Then sometimes an evangelist might misunderstand the problem. He might have someone demonstrate a healing by bending over to touch their toes when they didn't have a problem bending over in the first place. The audience wouldn't catch that and might believe that they had seen a miracle. Well, what was an honest mistake by the evangelist soon became a formula to resort to again and again if things weren't happening.

Eventually, most of the evangelists had wheelchairs available for people who had bad backs and couldn't stand in a healing line for hours. But when the evangelist got to them and pulled them up out of the wheelchair, some in the audience thought that they were walking for the first time or that they had come to the revival in that wheelchair.

An evangelist might have a vision one night that a prominent person in the audience is refusing to honor God by paying his tithes and that this man's refusal to honor God in this financial area of his life is jeopardizing his soul. Now the evangelist is very sincere. He is not trying to get money. He even tells the audience that their tithe belongs to their church, not to the evangelistic crusade. Then something remarkable happened. Maybe the prominent man in the audience is in a car accident, maybe he even dies, and his family comes to the evangelist with their story. It's real. It's just like the story of Ananias and Sapphira in the Bible. The man is dead.

The evangelist is naturally very impressed by what has happened. He starts telling the story in other towns. One night, he imagines that there is someone else in the audience in the same situation as this man. Is this thought from God, or is it his own imagination? A man's life may be at stake. He tells the audience. A man responds. "Yes, it's true. I am that man."

The evangelist finds that the offerings are almost triple when he tells this story—even though he is careful to tell the people that their tithe goes to their local church, not to himself. And the offerings triple again if he says, "There might be such a man here tonight." This evangelist has a budget. He has a dream to buy a bigger tent. It is all for God. Bingo— a formula is born. He may have crossed a line.

Now, I just used some hypothetical examples, but some things very close to that happened to some of the old *Voice of Healing* evangelists. This is what I mean by corruption. Usually, something very good, something very powerful, is the very thing that becomes corrupted.

Was this very common?

To one degree or another, every evangelist had to fight it. Now, don't get me wrong. In a sense, there is nothing wrong with developing a formula; God expects us to use our common sense and to learn from past experiences. Politicians, entertainers, salesmen, and athletes are all prepared for worst case scenarios and have fall-back plans. The comedian is prepared for a joke to flop, and he has a backup line to make fun of his own failure. In one sense, the traditional church is totally ritualized. Everything has become a formula. They can offer a rationale for anything. If there is no deliverance, no healing, no conversions, it doesn't matter. They can explain it all away.

Before the healing revival was all over, almost all the evangelists had developed a formula for their services. Some did so out of habit, some to provide a little "safety net" so that people would be blessed and not disappointed, and some may have crossed the line, believing that the ends justified the means. It became possible to conduct the whole service, even with apparent miracles—all without God.

Nothing did more to discredit the revival than this corruption. Most historians suggest that this was because the revival had reached a saturation point. We've talked before about how there wasn't enough money to go around. But I think it had something to do with the mounting pressure and competition among evangelists. The pressure came from audiences who had seen it all. They were jaded. Healing crossed eyes was nothing. Cancer? Well, that could remit naturally anyway. The lame walking? That could be a psychological cure. What else can someone do?

Remember when we talked about the rarity of a miracle? If it becomes common, it loses its power? In fact, when it becomes common, it ceases to become a miracle. That's what was beginning to happen. The revival was losing its miracles. The people were adjusting, even to beautiful manifestations of God's love. It was like the miracle of manna provided to the Israelis in the wilderness: "Isn't there anything else to eat?"

What happened to William Branham?

Well, ironically, he could have used a little more common sense and organization in his life. He remained a mystic to the end. There was never any financial corruption or sex scandal. But because of failing to keep adequate records, his organization found itself in all kinds of tax trouble with the government.

Branham resisted giving in to any kind of substitute for the very real moving of God. As a result, when he felt there was no healing power, he would just say so. His services became more unpredictable. There were more cancellations. Some felt that this was a moral failing, that his refusal to come to an announced meeting constituted the breaking of his word, his promise.

At times, when he refused to pray for the sick, he insisted on preaching for hours. One of my musicians was in such a meeting and said that it was so boring that he fell asleep three times in the middle of it. The Full Gospel Business Men had him in as a frequent speaker, but they paid him a pittance.

Over the years Branham had developed a cult following who were convinced that he was Elijah, the prophet returned to earth. It was the John Dowie phenomenon all over again. As Branham's popularity began to become eclipsed by Oral Roberts and others who were better organized, this little cult following finally found that they had Branham more and more to themselves. They greatly influenced him. Like Dowie, at the end, Branham was teaching some pretty weird things. Finally, he declared himself to be the angel of Revelation 3:14. In 1965, he died in an automobile accident. For some, it was an act of God's mercy to take him before he was influenced to do or say something even more controversial. By then, his name was already disappearing from the nation's consciousness. He left a humble man, with little money and very few speaking engagements. He had come full circle.

And Oral Roberts?

There was never the slightest hint of scandal about Oral Roberts, or even the people around him. This was a tribute to his superb organizational abilities and to his intelligence. He knew how controversial the healing message was. He had to be aware of how provocative it was becoming and how it was now attracting so many Christians on the fringe. He knew that the bureaucrats who worked in government agencies and the journalists who wrote for newspapers were human beings who belonged to other faiths or didn't have a faith at all. They didn't need much of an excuse to go after him. Some of the other evangelists could stir things up without much worry, but when they really started going after someone, Roberts, the big boy, knew that he was going to be the target. Even denominational Pentecostals had little power or prestige back then. They were despised, especially by other born-again Christians.

The Bible says that the badgers make their homes among the rocks and to learn that lesson. Roberts, perhaps sensing his vulnerability, and, no doubt, led by the Lord, began a new phase of his ministry. He launched Oral Roberts University and a new, mainstream television program that reached prime time audiences of millions. He identified more and more with the charismatic renewal in the traditional churches, even to the point of becoming a Methodist. It was quite a transformation.

And at the time, wasn't this greatly resented by his fellow Pentecostals?

Yes it was. I remember sitting with A.A. Allen as we watched the new Oral Roberts' television program. "Oh, Oral, you don't believe that," Allen would say. It was as if no one else were in the room but Allen and Roberts. "Come on, you can't kid me. You know better than that. Oral, Oral, we came out of the Methodist church, and now you're going back into it!" Of course, you know how bitterly Allen fought denominations.

Looking back on it, who can deny that Roberts made the right move? If the government or newspapers had gone after the revival, they would have targeted Oral Roberts, not the Assemblies of God, not the Pentecostal Holiness, or any other denomination. They had nothing to lose. Roberts did, and as a steward, he was responsible for it.

Perhaps the best proof of that was the harassment A.A. Allen went through. The I.R.S. hounded him unmercifully. In 1963, he finally went to court, and in a precedent-setting case, Allen kept his non-profit status.

But it was a close call, and it was expensive. Actually, he was fighting the battle for the non-profit status of all evangelistic organizations.

By any quantitative measurement, Oral Roberts won more to Christ and saw more miracles through his new ministry than he ever did through the old. I say that because his television audience was so much bigger. He had gone mainstream. Billy Graham dedicated his University. President Carter feted him around on Air Force I. George Bush had him in the Oval Office.

And yet there was the controversy of "God will take me home if I don't meet my budget."

Yes. But, you know, it was probably how Oral really felt. This was a big project, and he was feeling his age. He was tired of the burden, and his son, a successor, was in place. He may have been wondering why God still had him around. Great men have moments of self-doubt, just like the rest of us. Lost in the whole controversy was the fact that this was a very selfless project, one that involved young people going to desperately poor countries with medical help and humanitarian aid.

Also lost in the controversy was the fact that the Jim Bakker-Jimmy Swaggart scandal was on the front pages. If anyone else had made such a statement, it would have passed unnoticed. But Roberts was being monitored. His mailing list had been infiltrated by the media. They were looking for something to attack.

If Oral Roberts should pass from the scene today, I think the nation would have to put his whole career and life in perspective, and his integrity and business sense would dominate. I think it would be a huge front-page story about the impact he has had worldwide. There would be telegrams from heads of state. There would be a biography on *Arts and Entertainment*, and there would be a segment on *60 Minutes*.

But Oral Roberts isn't gone. He has shown an amazing resiliency. If he has taught us anything, he has taught us to be bold. To prepare thoroughly and then move quickly. Who knows what will still happen?

What about the others, T.L. Osborn and Gordon Lindsay?

Both of those men were men of integrity. Lindsay died in 1973, after founding Christ for the Nations, which is ably led to this day by his widow, Freda Lindsay. Over the years, she and her able organization have trained thousands and thousands of workers. And T.L. Osborn continues to minister around the world. He is older, and his ministry is much more selective than it was. Like all of us he has been somewhat eclipsed by the American televangelists, but he still has a powerful, very effective ministry.

When A.A. Allen died, T.L. Osborn was one of the few big evangelists who flew in to be with us. Understand, Allen was pretty much isolated by then. He made a career of taking the newspapers and the denominations head on. There was no reason for another evangelist to be associated with all that. But Osborn had a real love and appreciation for what God had done through all those men. He understood that they were just human beings and that they had faults, but he loved them just the same. We were all moved by the gesture.

Some of the evangelists just quit, didn't they?

Velmer Gardner and a couple of others bought a motel and got into businesses. Clifton Erickson went through a divorce, and for a time, he got a secular job in Denver. Later on, he got back into the ministry. Earl Ivy went blind. He used to come to our meetings and sit on the front row. You might remember David Walker, better known as "Little David" when he was a boy evangelist holding great citywide crusades. He's still in the ministry—pastoring a church. The great Tommy Hicks, the darling of the Full Gospel Business Men and who was a very gentle and kind man, developed a severe alcohol problem. He often came to Allen's Miracle Valley campus for prayer. In his great historic Argentina crusade, he had probably preached to the largest audience in the world, but he died unheralded, a very lonely man.

O.L. Jaggers, who was without a doubt the greatest orator in the whole bunch, just sort of faded away. He started teaching a doctrine that Christians would never die. I mean he taught that they would never die even a physical death. Of course, with each successive church funeral, the doctrine began to lose its credibility, and he began to lose his hold over his diminishing audience.

I remember him visiting Miracle Valley, Arizona. After the service, Allen had some of us younger ministers over to his house to visit with the man who had once been a legend in the healing revival. It was pitiful. Jaggers was very arrogant and condescending. He talked about the "city" he was building and how much of it was already finished. Of course, we knew that nothing was going on. His dream was over. But taking our cue from Allen, we were all kind to him. When he left, Allen said, "The problem is, boys, he really believes it."

Why did God allow that? If this was really a move of God, why didn't He let these great leaders pass from the scene with dignity? In their prime, they had been His servants. Why didn't He provide some personal vindication?

He took some home. Jack Coe, for example, died right in the middle of it. And others such as Kathryn Kuhlman took their lumps early and survived the whole period with their integrity intact. Believe me, I've given it all a lot of thought since I am sort of personally involved. Did all of these men and women fail? Did they become too proud? Could they have handled it differently?

Here's what I've concluded. I think God allowed some of these evangelists to outlive the revival to show that it really was a move of God's Spirit and not a creation of the men themselves. It was God, not those men. When the Spirit blew through, there was life and wonder, but after it passed, there was only a shell. Even Branham became a bore, with audiences falling asleep in his services. The things that happened—the healings, the miracles—were a demonstration of God's love for mankind. The evangelists, most of them poor, uneducated, abused sons of alcoholics, were only the unlikely vessels.

There was no second generation waiting to take over?

It's interesting that only a few of the sons or daughters were really able to pick up on their parents' healing ministry. If this were something that was just learned, if it were all formula, then one would expect Billy Paul Branham to carry on for his father. Perhaps we could expect one of Gordon Lindsay's sons to hit the sawdust trail. Yet that didn't happen.

Now, in some cases a ministry was "institutionalized" by the children and continued as a humanitarian outreach, a Bible school, or a church. In fact, this is what usually happened. I understand that Jack Coe, Jr., is ministering some now, but among the great healing evangelists there were very few sons or daughters to pick up the mantle and carry on the same type of ministry. Richard Roberts may be the best-known exception to the rule, although the Oral Roberts ministry is no longer exclusively a healing, evangelistic ministry. Richard Roberts is president of Oral Roberts University and, along with his wife, Lindsay, is ministering on television. According to some who know, Richard may be a better administrator than Oral Roberts was.

Yet there were a few younger evangelists coming to prominence as the revival tapered off.

Yes, in that sense, I would be considered a second generation healing evangelist. I was certainly much younger than all the others. There was also Leroy Jenkins, who only got started in 1960 and is still going.

Tell me about Jenkins. He seems to be a pretty hard one to explain. He is very controversial. There were reports that his ministry had problems with law enforcement. Yet journalists and others have checked him out, and they still report that there are miracles in his services.

Leroy Jenkins was healed in A.A. Allen's great Atlanta meeting in 1960. There were a number of miracles to come out of that crusade, but Jenkins' was the one that generated most of the excitement.

Jenkins came from a poor background and had very little education. But at a young age, he had attained a certain amount of success. Then he had an accident. A large plate glass window had broken, virtually severing his arm. The doctors determined that there was no way for the arm to heal properly, so they were planning to amputate. But Jenkins, who needed his job, begged them to try to save it. They sewed it back together, warning him that it wasn't going to heal and that they would have to amputate soon.

Now, understand this. The arteries and veins had been cut. To prevent him from bleeding to death they had painstakingly tied each of the blood vessels. It was a tedious, five-hour operation. So, there was no circulation in that arm. Likewise, the tendons had been cut. It was physically impossible for Jenkins to move his hand or fingers.

A.A. Allen was just daring and reckless in his faith. When he heard the story, he called Jenkins out of the audience, telling him that this was his night. I was the head usher that night, so I escorted Jenkins to the platform. Even before Allen started to pray, Jenkins began moving his hand and fingers. Well, there was pandemonium. Leroy Jenkins just stood there, raising his hands heavenward and crying with joy.

After a while, Allen handed Jenkins the microphone and told him to preach a little. Jenkins proceeded to tell the story of his accident and testified to his obvious miracle of healing. It brought the house down. Jenkins' ministry was launched immediately.

Over the next few days, doctors and friends confirmed just how miraculous the healing was. The doctors, who were still expecting to amputate the arm, were dumbfounded. Brother Allen began taking Jenkins to his crusades over the next few months and had him share the story of his amazing healing. The crowds always responded enthusiastically to the testimony.

Meanwhile, Leroy Jenkins was declaring that God had called him to preach. People wanted him to touch them with his "miracle arm." Within a few months, hundreds of others were claiming healings of every kind. It became inevitable that Jenkins would start his own crusades, so Allen gave him a send-off by giving him a tent to use in his first meetings. Without a doubt, Allen was very helpful in launching Jenkins into his own ministry.

Some of my staff who have worked for Oral Roberts, Kathryn Kuhlman, and many of the others claim that the miracles in Leroy Jenkins' meetings were the most spectacular of all. There may have been problems in his personal life, but no one can doubt the authenticity of the healings.

Were people "slain in the Spirit" or any other such phenomenon?

Jenkins started manifesting a gift similar to William Branham's. He could tell a stranger all about themselves. It was uncanny. And unlike Branham, Jenkins didn't get tired and wear out. He could go on for hours.

Was it a gimmick?

Oh no, it was very real. He could tell a person what he was thinking at that moment. That's not a gimmick. No prayer card or discreet assistant with a hidden microphone can make that happen. Jenkins would use this mystifying ability to tell people things about themselves and their physical problems. This seemed to motivate people to believe for their healings.

Eventually, Jenkins' unique gift captured the attention of some of Hollywood's rich and famous. They were intrigued by his unaffected, open personality; his dark, handsome good looks; and his extraordinary gift, which they identified as some sort of spiritual ESP. The legendary Mae West opened her Malibu Beach home to him and brought other luminaries to meet him at informal gatherings in the home. Through Jane Russell and her family, Jenkins ministered to famous stars, such as Liberace, Barbara Stanwyck, George Raft, and Mike Mazurki. Linda Evans and John Derek also attended his services. When Jenkins set up his tent in California, I've been told that many from the movie industry flocked to the meetings. They were fascinated with the showmanship he used in presenting his ministry.

What about the miracles?

One of my associates, Bob Daniels, worked with Leroy Jenkins as the crusade director back in the late 1960's. Daniels said that Jenkins was fearless and bold with his faith for healing. Just like his mentor, A.A. Allen, Jenkins put his ministry on the line. And almost every time that he prayed for a difficult, apparently impossible miracle of healing, God seemed to honor his "holy daring."

In 1964, Jenkins started a tent crusade in Pensacola. Only 75 people showed up that first night. In that large tent that seated thousands and seemed cavernous, this very tiny group of people barely outnumbered the staff. Members of the Jenkins team thought they should close the meetings and move someplace where his ministry was better known. But Jenkins took the pitiful crowd as a challenge to prove God was with him.

A lady by the name of Willie Blackwell was in the meeting who had a bandage covering most of her right cheek. Jenkins called her out of the audience and told Mrs. Blackwell that the Lord had shown him there was a cancer on her face. He asked her if she would mind if he took the bandage off to "take a peek at that thing." The removal of the bandage revealed an ugly, gray-looking growth. It was red around the edges and about the size of a half dollar.

Jenkins took some Kleenex tissues in his hand and placed them over the growth, praying: "Lord, if I be Your servant, I ask You to let this foul thing fall off in my hand. And God, if I'm not Your servant, then I ask You not to let it be removed—in the name of Jesus." You have to admit, that pretty well lays it all on the line for your ministry.

When he took his hand away, Bob Daniels says that the entire ugly growth was now in the tissues in Jenkins' hand. It had been completely removed, leaving a large, open sore on the side of Mrs. Blackwell's face. The small crowd went absolutely wild. From that night forward, the attendance grew dramatically. The meeting closed out with the giant tent full and hundreds of people standing outside.

Jenkins assured Mrs. Blackwell that the hole in her face would fill in and heal in time, and it did. Some months later, Mrs. Blackwell returned to one of Leroy Jenkins' crusades in Daytona Beach, Florida. The skin had healed over completely, and only a small pink dot remained as testimony to the miracle of healing. Mrs. Blackwell said that her healing had given her the opportunity to testify in churches all over the area about God's miraculous healing power.

There were countless miracles of healing that he personally witnessed in Jenkins' meetings, but Daniels states that this healing stands out because it was highly visible and dramatic. It generated a lot of "word of mouth" publicity that resulted in large, enthusiastic crowds for subsequent crusades across Florida. People came to Jenkins' meetings in anticipation of what might happen next.

And, yet, his ministry did not explode on the scene like Branham's or Allen's.

Remember, Jenkins was uneducated, and some say that he didn't know his Bible. The accusation was that he wouldn't submit to any teaching about Scripture. Others say that Jenkins didn't use wisdom in operating his gift. He would challenge people who were skeptics and say something like this, "You don't believe this is God? Come up here. I'll show you." And if they wouldn't come up, he would say something like, "You're nothing but a coward." But if they did come up, Jenkins would generally amaze them by describing perfectly some hidden scar on their body, or tell them what brand of cigarettes they smoked and exactly how many were left in the pack. It really shook people up.

Yet Jenkins was pleased with the way things were going. Why should he listen to someone else? He may not have had a formal education, but he certainly had a keen intellect. He was intuitively smart. His crowds were big. The finances were easy. He didn't really need an organization. He would come to town with a tent, start with 50 people, and have a couple of thousand in his audience within a few days.

Branham had put together a team of highly credible men: F.F. Bosworth, Gordon Lindsay, and others. Leroy Jenkins, on the other hand, seemed to be leery of trusting his fate to an organization. From time to time, Jenkins put together a credible team and enjoyed some national prominence. But then he would fire everyone and change direction. Maybe he feared that he might lose control or was unsure about trusting others. It was almost as if he didn't want to get too big. Perhaps because he didn't really want the responsibility that goes with it.

There were a lot of very damaging rumors about his personal life.

I don't really know anything about his personal life. Jenkins crusaded against the hypocrisy in the Church. In a fashion similar to the

California television preacher, Gene Scott, Jenkins would use a few spicy words in his speech, even in his sermons. Jenkins had no pretenses. He let his audiences know that he was human. Through the years this attracted a rather unique audience that really loved him. But it also created controversy and closed the doors to ministries in the churches.

He was brutally honest, and if he thought something, he generally said it or did it. I attended one of Jenkins' meetings recently and he told his audience a story that would shock most people. Jenkins related an incident about a woman who became angry with him in one of his meetings. She got so mad that she reached out and slapped his face. Jenkins said, "Well, I just slapped her back as hard as I could. So don't even try to do that to me." The audience got his point.

Some critics have written Jenkins off as an arrogant rebel, who is rashly impetuous and impatient, too colorful, and very "show-bizzy." But those who have worked closely with him through the years describe him differently. He can be demanding and unpredictable, but at the same time he can be considerate, generous, loyal, and fun-loving to an almost childish degree. His charming Southern accent and personality can disarm people. He cannot tolerate discrimination or abuse, and he reacts angrily to anyone who he believes is trying to manipulate or use him for his or her own selfish gain. Someone said, "He'll fight you for a nickel, but will give the shirt off his back."

Why did God give him such gifts? Why not give them to some very holy, devout person with biblical knowledge and a strong sense of humility?

Very much like William Branham, Jenkins feels that he received the gift when he was born. Who can explain it? Nobody deserves such gifts. Nobody is good enough for them—nobody, not you or I, not the Pope. Why not Leroy Jenkins?

The whole story is a real object lesson for understanding the grace and mercy of God. And then, there is God's extravagance. One can walk into the middle of a forest and find beautiful flowers that no person on earth will ever see but you.

Even today, Leroy Jenkins is still ministering across the country. Although the crowds are not what they used to be, they are witnessing amazing miracles that are just as real as those of the great healing revivals of the 1950's. I recently went to one of his services in New York. Jenkins called a man out of the audience and told him what brand of cigarettes he had in a pocket inside his coat. Believe me, you couldn't see inside the coat. Jenkins told him how many cigarettes he had left. Then he had the man take the pack out and count the remaining cigarettes. It was exactly what Jenkins had said. It was pretty impressive. It will make you wonder if maybe you ought to pay attention to whatever else the man has to say.

Then there was the problem with the law. Didn't he burn someone's house down? It was something pretty outrageous.

You're referring to Jenkins' conviction and incarceration back in 1979. But like any story, there are two sides to tell. According to the actual newspaper accounts, opinions about guilt or innocence were pretty well split along the lines of a well-planned "sting" against Jenkins by locals through the means of the government.

Jenkins was living in Greenwood, South Carolina, at that time. From all accounts, the local authorities, some from churches who didn't believe in healing, were not enamored with Jenkins' success and popularity. Members of Jenkins' staff told me that from the very beginning, signs of jealousy and resentment materialized in the opposition of certain city officials to Jenkins' efforts to relocate his international offices in their sleepy little town. He thoroughly antagonized the powers that be when he announced plans to establish another newspaper by saying: "Every town ought to have two papers, and at least one that will tell the truth." But, I was told, the thing that really got the locals heated up was when Jenkins announced his decision to run for mayor when the next election came around.

Now, here's where the so-called "Billy Murphy" enters the picture. He was an employee of one of Jenkins' sub-contractors in Greenwood. He was eager to be of service, willing to help with any task no matter how big or little. But he was not what he appeared to be. "Billy Murphy" was actually Agent Bruce Mirkin, sent by the Bureau of Alcohol, Tobacco, and Firearms to get close to Jenkins. He wore a concealed tape recorder, hoping to record and expose any possible illegal activity Jenkins might be engaged in.

However, Jenkins didn't give Mirkin anything to report to his government bureau that could be used to discredit his ministry. That is, nothing until Jenkins' teenage daughter had been manhandled and arrested by the police for exceeding the speed limit and driving without her license when she drove to a McDonald's for a hamburger. After getting his daughter Candy out of jail late at night and hearing her story of being dragged in handcuffs from the McDonald's to the police station, Jenkins was irate, and Mirkin played on his anger.

According to Jenkins, Mirkin offered to "get that patrolman for you." Mirkin said: "I'm a torch. I'll burn down his house for you." In the course of their conversation, Jenkins commented that he would "like to knock the block off" a local newspaper reporter. Of course, this was recorded on the agent's hidden tape recorder. Those words, uttered in anger in the privacy of his home, formed the basis for a charge by the state that Jenkins was conspiring to beat up the reporter and burn the home of the highway patrolman. It appears to have been the idea and suggestion of the agent at all times.

The facts are that no crime had been committed, no one's home burned, and no one was ever assaulted. According to Jenkins, he never had any intention to commit any of these acts. But the city fathers of Greenwood had what they wanted. Jenkins was in custody. His attorneys were denied a continuance to prepare properly for his defense. The rush to judgment resulted in a verdict of "guilty" and Jenkins was sentenced to 20 years in prison, reduced to 12 years.

Everyone I've talked to who was present at the trial declares that Jenkins was set up and then railroaded. The powers that be, including some of the religious leaders, seemed determined to bring his ministry down by any means whatsoever. It was a terrible tragedy, and it may have been a travesty of justice.

Jenkins spent four long, hard years in prison, but he has always maintained that he was set up by the local authorities in Greenwood. The trial got quite a bit of national attention, and the famed defense attorney F. Lee Bailey even offered to handle an appeal of Jenkins' conviction.

In 1983, Jenkins was paroled after agreeing that he would leave South Carolina and never return. This agreement, in itself, could be interpreted as an obvious indication of the source and reason for the charges against him. It looks like authorities in Greenwood wanted to get rid of Leroy Jenkins any way they could. With the aid of a "planted" federal agent, they succeeded.

How did it happen? How can someone go from the ministry to prison?

In part, it was a result of isolation. Jenkins and many of the other evangelists were cut off from any fellowship with the churches and other ministers. Everyone needs that. The Bible talks about it. An anointed ministry that is operating in the gifts of the Spirit has to have an atmosphere of freedom to be effective. Yet it can be a two-edged sword. There needs to be some form of accountability.

And A.A. Allen? What happened to him during those years of isolation? How did he function without any denominations in authority above him?

Well, in one sense he had his greatest ministry after he left the denomination. I don't necessarily believe that just because a person is in a denomination that it will keep a minister from having problems. Both Jim Bakker and Jimmy Swaggart were in denominations. In fact, when they had all their trouble, both organizations were members of the Evangelical Council for Financial Accountability (E.C.F.A.).

I think the most important thing is that you have someone around you who can be trusted and who loves you and your ministry. You need someone who will tell you what he really believes, not what he thinks you want to hear. You need someone for checks and balances, to help you stay on track and not lose touch. For some, it may be a denomination. For others, it may be a group of their peers, a few ministers, or a few close, trusted friends whom they can bounce things off of to get direction and keep focus.

We talked earlier about the tendency for long-time evangelists to reduce their services to a formula. Did Allen struggle with that?

Oh, I'm sure he did. But he didn't give in to it. He continually stepped back from crossing that line. For example, Allen liked to meet the people who were coming for prayer. They would come to an afternoon service before the main event, and he liked to talk to them and get a sense of their faith. If he felt they were ready and that they had faith, he would pray for them first. If there were one or two outstanding miracles at the beginning of the service, then faith would rise in the audience, and all kinds of things began to happen.

Well, after talking to those people, he knew things about them. It would have been very easy for him that night to leave the impression with the audience that he was receiving this information from the Lord in a supernatural way. The Allen team would have thought that the audience was only misunderstanding. They loved and respected Allen. They never would have suspected him of manipulating the audience. Allen could have gotten away with it. But he was very, very careful. If he noticed that the audience was getting the wrong idea, he would correct it. "This was not supernaturally revealed to me," he would say. "I met this person in the prayer tent this afternoon. We talked about this."

It would have been the easiest thing in the world to let the audience think what it wanted to think and so enhance his legend, but he didn't do it.

What about situations when it may have appeared that a miracle had happened, but in fact it really wasn't as spectacular as it seemed?

Kathryn Kuhlman rented hundreds of wheelchairs for her big crusades, where thousands of people waited for hours to get in. Sometimes she didn't stop the service to explain that the person being wheeled to the front in a wheelchair was only someone with back trouble. It may not have been the miracle that some in the audience supposed, but that happened accidentally. It was not part of some formula. I can understand it. It happens in my own ministry. There are times that things are happening so fast that you can't stop to qualify what has happened or explain all the details.

We talked about Allen's drinking problem earlier. Were there occasions when this problem would surface?

I'm not comfortable talking about it. As far as I am concerned, A.A. Allen was a man of God and should be respected for that. This part of his life was deeply, deeply personal. Yes, it was a struggle. But all men and women have struggles. Some struggle with gluttony or lust, some with pride or greed. People of faith are not immune to that sort of thing. Abraham had his struggles. David committed murder and adultery, but he was considered a man after God's own heart. Peter denied the Lord and God still used him.

And yet, refusing to talk about it only leads to greater misunderstandings. This is essentially an historical account. If someone is sincerely seeking to understand what God did during these years, they should know a little bit about how these men dealt with their weaknesses.

I guess you are right because everyone has weaknesses. Yes, there were occasional relapses. Allen would go for months without an incident, and then he would disappear for a few days and we would have to carry on without him.

I remember once coming to the platform of a service and finding that Allen had drunk too much. He didn't look out of line. He was well-dressed and was comporting himself decently, but he was slurring his words and, up close, you could tell that he was just out of it.

Now, people on his staff were afraid of him, and they deeply respected him. He was very strong, and they held him in awe. However, I was like a son to him. He felt that he could trust me. Even though I held him in awe, I could talk to him straight in a way that others on the team could not. I said, "Brother Allen, I want you to know that I love you and I make no judgment against you, but you are in no condition to run this service. We can handle it. Let's get you to your room right now and get you to bed."

He was as meek as a lamb. "You're right," he said. And I put him in my car and took him to his room.

Yet he denied his problem?

We all did. We just ignored it. The next day no one would say a word. It was between him and the Lord. We all had such great respect for him; we didn't want to hurt him. We loved him. He was like a father to me.

Yet that denial was wrong.

Yes. It was the one area where we all woke up one day and found ourselves on the other side of that proverbial line.

In my heart of hearts I don't believe that he set out to deceive anybody. Remember, after the DUI incident in Knoxville, he met with Assemblies of God officials, and they gave him the promise that they would deal with the incident quietly and privately as any church would. Then, one of the presbyters immediately leaked the whole thing to the newspapers. What I didn't tell you was the nature of the leak. What he told the newspapers was that Allen was guilty and that he was going to publicly admit it at a news conference the next day.

Of course, Allen was stunned. The ruthless nature of the betrayal was mind-boggling to him. His first instinct, out of anger and out of survival, I suppose, was to deny it. Now, some have said that he was denying the Assemblies statement that he was going to hold a press conference to admit to it or that he was denying the newspaper account because so many parts of it weren't accurate. The members of his own evangelistic team fiercely defended him. Afterward, he just kept silent or said things to deflect the attack.

If someone attacked him he might answer, "They called Jesus a drunkard and a wine bibber too." This response, of course, implied that he was innocent, just as Jesus was innocent. Once he denied it, he was caught in a trap.

That was wrong?

Yes.

How did his own staff rationalize it?

Most of them really believed in his innocence, which made it even worse. They hotly defended him to one and all. The publishers of his magazine called it a "conspiracy of communists and Catholics." When they were confronted with evidence of the DUI, they said that he had been kidnapped and that alcohol had been poured down his throat to fake it—that he was framed.

There were those few who, over the years, became aware of the fact that he really had a problem and were able to put it into context. Here was a man who was preaching almost nightly. His whole life was committed to God. He didn't snow ski, he didn't play baseball, he hardly ever watched television, and he never told a dirty joke. He gave his life to the poorest people of the country. He was casting out demons and healing the sick. Thousands were saved. If he had a problem, it was under control.

In some respects, compared to some of the televangelist scandals of today, scandals involving prostitutes or money, Allen's occasional lapses seem almost tame. As you pointed out, the same Scriptures that talk against drunkenness also talk about gluttony and other problems. But there is the contradiction that Allen publicly preached against alcohol. And he was tough on the subject. Then there were the public denials within his own magazine, which he could have corrected. How do you think Allen himself rationalized it?

I know for a fact that he went through a personal hell each time he relapsed. He would pray something like, "God, if I can't accept Your deliverance for myself, how can I stand up in front of other people and believe it for them?" He repented and sincerely felt that it would never happen again. Sadly, he had learned the lesson that there was not a single person on earth he could trust. Any outside counseling was out of the question. He would decide that it was "under the blood." God had forgiven him, and as the Scripture says, He had forgotten about it, and

Allen should do the same. Only satan would try to accuse him. The Bible says that satan is "the accuser of the brethren" (see Rev. 12:9-10). Since it was over with and done, it was as if it didn't happen.

But it did happen?

Yes. There were a few relapses. But given his childhood and background, it was nothing less than a miracle that he was able to reach up and believe God to help him. I have a great amount of respect for his ability to never give up. It reminds me of what Theodore Roosevelt said: "The credit belongs to the man who is actually in the arena, whose face is marred by dust and sweat and blood; who strives valiantly, who errs and comes short again and again. Who knows the great enthusiasms, the great devotions, and spends himself in a worthy cause. Who at best knows the triumph of high achievement and who at the worst, if he fails, at least fails while daring greatly, so that his place shall never be with those cold and timid souls who know neither victory nor defeat."

There was a lot of controversy surrounding his death. The final word from the coroner had him dying of acute alcoholism. You don't still deny that now, do you?

No. But by the same token, his life should be viewed in its context and not by the more sensational episodes that were rare occurrences.

And yet, this denial of the problem only arouses more curiosity and attention. I think people would be willing to examine his life in its context if there was less duplicity and evasiveness about his problems. The Bible is full of great men who did great exploits, but it doesn't hesitate to talk about their struggles. There is a learning process here.

For years people would ask me about A.A. Allen's death, and I would answer, "What difference does it make; he was a man of God. All I know is that he pointed me to everything that was good and away from anything that was bad."

That doesn't answer the question.

No, it doesn't, but I was very sincere. He was a godly man. I've never known a more dedicated man to God and his ministry than him. The story of his death has never really been told, and I suppose, if the next generation is going to have a complete understanding of this healing revival era, someone should finally tell what happened. In fact, I may be the only one who can tell it, since I was the one who was there.

Allen had been depressed for some time. Maybe the work was finally getting to him. There were enormous financial pressures. He may have tired with his "thorn in the flesh," his personal problem. Then he was suffering greatly from arthritic spurs in his knees. Seeking medical help was a humiliating experience for him. However, the pain had become unbearable.

You see, Allen had always preached that when illnesses come, we should just trust God to deliver us. Turning to doctors was "trusting the arm of the flesh"; that is, looking for natural answers to problems instead of looking to God. Allen had even written a book about it. He used the scriptural account of King Asa. The Bible says that he had "trusted the arm of the flesh" and his kingdom was cursed because of it (see 2 Chron. 16:7-12). Well, Asa Alonso Allen, who had the same name as the Old Testament king, must have identified with him. Now, here he was, contradicting his own teaching. He was going to doctors for help. Would he be cursed as well?

I remember he came to me very quietly after a revival in Mobile, Alabama. He told me that he wanted my help to get him to a doctor in San Francisco. He was emphatic that I not tell a soul—not his sister, his children, or any of his other associates. This was very awkward, since his family had every right to know. Still, I did as he requested. I helped him arrange for the operation and checked him into the hospital in San Francisco. Then I flew on to Birmingham, Alabama, to help start the next crusade. We had three services a day back then, with Gene Martin and Kent Rogers helping to carry the load.

After Birmingham we went on to Cincinnati. Allen was anxious to get back into the pulpit. Yet the operation had left him in great pain. Today, with lasers and endoscopic instruments, the surgery isn't as serious, but then, it was somewhat complicated. The whole experience had left him deeply depressed and physically drained. So, I agreed to bring him into Cincinnati, and that last weekend against all my entreaty, he insisted on taking the service. He was in great pain. He shouldn't have been out of bed. He could barely walk. But when he started singing his theme song, "Where the roses never fade," he seemed to gain strength. He preached a powerful sermon, he prayed for the sick that night, and there were outstanding miracles. He never preached again.

From there we went to Wheeling, West Virginia. He was now exhausted from the pain. He had overused his legs in Cincinnati, so he couldn't do anything. He stayed in his house trailer next to the tent. He could hear everything that went on. I preached that night and prayed for the sick. God gave me a special anointing. It was a beautiful service.

The next day I went into his trailer. He was reading his Bible and he handed it to me. "Don, I want you to read this." It was the second chapter of Ecclesiastes. When I finished he just stood there for a long time and then he said, "Now, Don, read the eighteenth verse and tell me what that means."

I didn't know what he was talking about. Of course, I can see it all now. The verse said, "I hated all the things I had toiled for under the sun, because I must leave them to the one who comes after me" (NIV). I just shrugged.

Later, that moment haunted me. I think he had mixed emotions about my own success, the success of R.W. Shambach, and that of some of his other former associate evangelists. On the one hand, he loved us dearly. He was proud of us all. On the other hand, he may have begun to feel unneeded. He actually said that several times. "I'm not needed around here anymore." Allen was very generous, willing to use the ministry's money to promote and develop other evangelists. That last night in Wheeling, he had listened to the meeting from the trailer. It was all going to go on without him. He may have felt that he would be forgotten. If so, he was wrong. No one could ever take his place.

He said, "Don, I want you to take me to Pittsburgh. I'm going to catch a plane back to San Francisco to see the doctor."

I had Jimmy Vickers drive us to Pittsburgh. Right up to the last minute I urged Allen to take me along. "Please, Brother Allen," I said, "let me go with you. Kent Rogers and Gene Martin can keep the meeting going."

But he was insistent. "No, Don, that's your job. You're the one who can carry the meeting."

"It will only be a couple of days. I can be back in time to close out the weekend."

"No." He was very firm.

Perhaps I had a premonition. He was very depressed. I stayed right with him all the way to the gate. I put my arms around him and told him how much I loved him.

"Don," he said, "you have been very loyal to me, and that makes you a very big man in my eyes. You are ready. Just follow God, and you will do a great job." I felt very humbled by his words. Then he boarded his plane and never looked back.

That evening I called him from Wheeling, West Virginia. It was about 6:00 p.m. our time, just before the start of the evening service. He answered the phone in his room at the Jack Tar Hotel in San Francisco. He sounded very bad, very depressed. "I can come out there," I said, but again he said, "No." Instinctively, I knew that something serious was going on, although I couldn't imagine what it could be. It was just a gut feeling. I left the meeting and had Jimmy Vickers drive me to Pittsburgh to catch a plane.

While changing planes at O'Hare airport in Chicago I called again. His voice was weak, and he slurred his words. I told him that I was coming out there and that I was on my way.

When I finally got to the hotel I obtained a key to the room and raced down the hall. But I was too late. He was gone. There were empty vodka bottles all over the room. I shut the door and cried: "You can't leave me this way. I love you. I'm not ready to handle all the responsibility. You cared for me when no one else cared. You saw something in me when no one else did."

I think I felt like the disciples did when Christ died—together in a room with the door closed, feeling helpless and hopeless, because their King was gone. To me, Reverend A.A. Allen was the ultimate. He was Paul and Peter. He was Moses and Joshua. He was God's man of faith and power.

I can't begin to describe the emotions that surged through me in that hotel room. A thousand memories flooded my mind. The introduction that I gave him every night kept playing over and over in my head. "Ladies and gentlemen, it is my very happy pleasure and privilege to present to you the man that God has raised up with a supernatural, miracle-working ministry, spearheading the restoration revival across America and around the world—God's man of faith and power—A.A. Allen." But now he was gone.

How many souls had he won to the Lord? It had to be in the millions. Night after night, thousands would flood the altars. How many times had I seen him filled with compassion, weeping over the people in the healing line, lifting a cripple up off the stretcher, ordering demons out of some crazy person whom the psychiatrists had given up on. Holding a little cross-eyed child in his arms, and not giving up until he saw the eyes straighten. He never shrank back from the worst cases, the invalids whom other ministers avoided. And the poor...how he loved the poor, and how they loved him.

This was a great man of God, a worker who preached twice a day for months back to back without even an afternoon off. Some mornings I would find him praying and studying his Bible until 4:00 a.m. He would never let us say a negative word about another preacher. He had given me hope and confidence when no one else really believed in me. I wasn't about to let him die like this. I scooped up all the vodka bottles into a trash bag and slipped out a side door of the Jack Tar Hotel, throwing the whole thing into a dumpster. Then I came back, tidied up the room, and started making calls.

The first one was to our lawyer. "I don't care what it takes," I said. "Let's let this man die with some dignity." So the lawyer and I consulted with the doctor, and he agreed to delay the final autopsy report as long as he could—until the report had to be officially filed. The first story out of San Francisco said that Allen had died with apparent "heart attack-like symptoms," which was technically true. That got us through the funeral.

When the autopsy finally came in several weeks later, it showed that he had died of acute alcoholism. The story was flashed across the country. But, thankfully, for the family and those who loved him, many people never picked up on it. So, his death was not turned into a media scandal, and he was able to pass from the scene with a measure of dignity.

Finally, for the record, that's what really happened.

Chapter Eight

The Last of the Healing Evangelists

Don Stewart

In January 1996, I was on a speaking tour across Asia when I got a call from Don Stewart. Would I want to fly over to the Philippines and take in a crusade? From what I had read and heard, the healing revival of the 1950's had never waned in this beautiful country. Here was a rare opportunity, a window through which I could take yet another look at the spiritual awakening that had so impacted the Pentecostal movement of the previous generation.

In between the marathon of afternoon and evening services, Don and I sat down to talk about what was happening and how the healing ministry was ongoing in many countries around the world.

* * *

Let's talk about the blind lady in Koronondahl, the very first one you prayed for. That set the tone of the whole crusade. Why her?

The truth is I don't know. In a situation like that, the evangelist is led of the Holy Spirit. He is operating with spiritual instinct. This elderly lady was near the front, and she was blind in one eye. The people around her had gotten my attention. They wanted me to pray for her. Such a miracle would surely be a dramatic demonstration of God's power. It was a good way to get started.

The reverse is also true. If she had not been healed, you would have had to spend the rest of the week digging yourself out of a hole. This was the defining moment. Most of your audience had never seen you before. They were wondering about all this—whether it was for real or not. And, in a sense, you were trusting this person you had never met, this old woman. Who was she? This was a remote region of the Philippines. She could have been into witchcraft for all you knew, which might have hindered her healing. It seemed very risky.

Well, first of all, I was not trusting that old lady; I was trusting God and His Word. In a time like that, you cannot hesitate or doubt, or you have no business up there. You have to believe. You cannot be calculating which is the safest case to pray over, which one can be explained if there is no immediate result, or which disease is the most psychological and therefore the most likely to be healed. Believe me, the audience is thinking those things. They were just as shocked as you were. This was not what they expected.

And yet, we have been talking about the methods and patterns of healing evangelists. You said that A.A. Allen, Oral Roberts, and others often met the persons they prayed for even before the service. This allowed them to identify people with faith, people who were believing God for a miracle. You said that this had been your own method, and yet in Korononadahl, you violated it. You picked a person at random. What would you have said or done when she hadn't been healed?

Earlier I used prayer cards, but in the past 20 years, I've found that I operate best in spontaneous situations like this. If you remember this particular incident, at first the lady wasn't completely healed. She said that she saw light. Now that's something. She had been totally blind in that eye. The audience went crazy. That was enough for them. As far as they were concerned, this was a miracle already. At that point, I could have praised God and rushed her off the platform, and we would have been off and running. But I could see that she was not satisfied. Her expectations were really up. So I reminded the audience of the time that Jesus prayed for the blind man who later said, "I see men, but they look like trees" (see Mk. 8:24). He prayed again, and the blind man could see perfectly. So I prayed again, and this time the lady could see.

That was what you called the "defining moment." When the old woman saw light, there had been a huge reaction from the audience, but when I prayed the second time and she could see out of that eye and started leaping up and down, well, that's when it all started happening.

That's a rather mild description. Actually, there was pandemonium. People rushed the stage. The reports of healings from the audience started coming faster than your people could keep track.

Well, you must understand, most Christians, even those who believe in miracles, will never see a blind eye instantly open. They may hear a testimony, but they will not personally see it happen—never. That night it happened again and again.

When the woman said she saw light, the audience thought, *Wow, this is powerful stuff, this is real.* They were expecting people to limp on and limp off, with lots of theological explanations about why their faith wasn't good enough or that the results sometimes come later. When I prayed again and she could really see, they thought, *Wait a minute, this really happened.*

At that point, I was wanting you to slow down, to talk to these people longer, to verify the miracles by getting more information. There were so many testimonies of healings, one right after the other. There was no way to get to them all. Why not focus more on the most outstanding?

Well, we do that. My staff is there getting all the details and following up. And as you know, I do some of that on stage in front of the audience, but there are thousands of people in the audience who want prayer too. We can't just stop and spend the evening interviewing people. Besides, after a few minutes in an interview, you have done all that you can do. For any more verification there must be X-rays or medical reports, and that comes later, after the person makes a visit to his or her doctor. As a matter of fact, the biggest miracles to come out of a meeting like that are usually not known until afterward when someone writes in with all the documentation. There are just too many people in the audience, and some can't or won't come to the front to report their healing.

The same thing happened in Roxas City. The first person you prayed for was a man who had suffered a stroke.

That's right. He was paralyzed on one side of his body. As I remember, he couldn't move one of his arms. His hands and fingers didn't work, and to get around he needed a walker. I prayed for him. God healed him.

And the place went wild.

Well, people hunger for a visible demonstration of God's power. They know about it and believe it, but sometimes they have to see it. That's why the first one I pick is usually someone blind, or deaf, or someone who has a goiter—something visible. People say to themselves, *I believe that God heals the sick, but He does it naturally or gradually. He wouldn't just heal someone instantly*. So some need an example that's visible.

In this case, the man raised his hands to praise God, and at the same time he suddenly realized that he could use his paralyzed arm. He started weeping with joy, and that set the audience off. They could see the man's reaction. They knew that he was healed, and again, the reports of answered prayers started coming as fast as we could keep track of them.

There was no fund-raising or even an offering in Roxas City. Why? It's impressive. But how do you pay for the crusade?

Good question. A crusade like that is very expensive, but in this case it was entirely underwritten by a close friend, a woman who had been healed in one of my earlier crusades. There were not very many evangelical Christians in this community, and we wanted to come as givers, not takers. You will remember that thousands of people came forward for salvation, maybe 30 percent of the audience.

I believe in taking offerings. People should have a chance to give, to show God that they are submitted in every area of their life, including their finances. Tithing is a very important doctrine. But this was the time to give freely to the people. There should never be any misunderstanding. You cannot buy a healing from God. He responds to faith, and He doesn't heal because you are good or righteous. He heals out of love. His gifts are given freely.

By the same token, I should say something here that will make a lot of people uncomfortable, but it is the truth. I have witnessed tremendous miracles, even healings, in the lives of people who gave very sacrificially to the Lord. Perhaps it does something to our own faith when we humble ourselves before the Lord and do something material or substantial for Him. He has to be Lord of our finances too.

Now go back with me to Korononadahl. After the blind lady, there were several women in a row who were healed of goiters. Why so many goiters?

It's interesting. There are some regions of the Philippines where goiters are very common. Maybe it has something to do with the water or the diet.

This will sound like a stupid question, but are goiters easier to heal? Is there something psychosomatic about it? That week there were so many healings of goiters. How do you explain that?

I have seen so many goiters disappear that I probably have more faith to call for such healings. And again, here is something visible. If I pray for someone with leukemia, they may say, "I feel different." Or they will say, "I think I'm healed; I felt something like an electric shock go through me." And maybe they are healed. But we won't know until they have had blood tests. But with a goiter, it is pretty clear to everyone. Where did it go? It was there a minute ago. The whole audience could see it. Where did it go?

Well, I wanted to ask you about that too. No one can deny that the goiters are gone. Does the body absorb them? Is it possible that they shrink or maybe just move deeper into the body? And then another question: Do they come back later?

Look. Some of those goiters were hanging from their necks like basketballs. In reality, the goiter itself is probably the size of a billiard ball. But with the pocket of skin around it and in that location on the neck, they appear huge. The point is that they are visible. They're hard to miss. Then, suddenly, they are gone. There is just loose skin hanging from the neck. Accept it. You saw it with your own eyes. That's what we call a miracle.

They don't move deeper into the body, that's for sure. The person would know it. They can feel it when they swallow. A goiter is very constrictive. If it only moved deeper inside the neck, the person would be choking.

One of the more poignant moments in the crusade was to see that whole row of ladies, who had been healed of goiters, sitting there with their friends quietly weeping with joy. Their friends were looking on, amazed that the goiters were no longer visible. And the ladies who had been healed were probing with their fingers, trying to feel if there was even a little bit left.

Let's talk about the doctor's wife. She had two goiters and a tumor on her hip, and all three just disappeared.

As a matter of fact, this was more likely the "defining moment," as you put it, in the crusade. You will remember that there was a gasp from the audience when she identified herself. The community knew her. Her husband was the chief surgeon in the local hospital, and there she was, on stage, testifying to the healing power of God and what had happened to her. Her husband examined her and confirmed it all.

I wondered about that reaction. First, the audience was amazed when the blind lady could see light. Then, there was a bigger reaction when she started seeing perfectly. It was as if they didn't expect it. There was also the reaction to the doctor's wife. Here is somebody they knew personally from their community. This person couldn't be faking. The people knew where she lived, and her husband was a prominent member of their community. But the audience reaction still betrays a skepticism, for in each case they were surprised.

Well, you know what? I'm surprised too, and I'm the evangelist. That's what makes it a miracle. It isn't supposed to happen. I'm amazed no matter how often I see it.

These people are not non-believers, if that's what you are implying. The hardened skeptics usually stay home. They don't bother to come unless they are investigating the subject or have some obsessive curiosity. Most people are too busy. They have things to do. The majority of the people who come are people who either believe or want to believe. They are sick, or their loved ones are sick. They want a miracle.

Now, it's true that most in that audience are not really born again. That's true. Since the days of Jesus, healing ministries have always attracted the non-religious. But that night, I had already preached the Word. Many had already accepted Christ, and many Christians were there in the audience. They had been praying for months. There was a huge Catholic population in the city, and the Catholics in the audience believe in miracles. So there was an atmosphere of faith.

And yet, you kept singling people out for prayer, seemingly the most difficult cases. Isn't that risky? At that point, why not just

focus on the healings that have already taken place and bring them up out of the audience? There were hundreds of those.

Well, we did that too. But you have to understand, I'm not in the business of putting on a show. I'm not there just to play it safe. I'm in the business of helping people. I'm in the business of faith. This was the tradition of A.A. Allen. I suppose that I got it from him. He would always go after the most hopeless case. And he would stay to help as many as he could. He never said, "Wow, that last one was good—let's quit while we're ahead," and then leave the others behind.

Risky? True. I wouldn't recommend that some Bible school student get up and try it. But the reward is that much greater because the people can't easily explain it away. If I reduce it to a formula where only those who are already healed are brought forward, well, the audience can see that. They aren't dumb. They wouldn't blame me for that; they are still miracles, and they glorify God. Yet when I put everything on the line like that, it becomes that much more powerful when something happens. Many will accept it for what it is, a miracle of God. It becomes a faith builder.

Does it ever backfire? Obviously, every person you single out for prayer doesn't get healed?

Sure it backfires. Many I pray for don't get healed. A long time ago I made this deal with God: I won't take the credit for the people You heal. But I don't get blamed for the ones You don't heal.

That next night the doctor came back with several other doctors with him. Is that common?

That's very typical. If you will notice, all the dynamics we have been talking about were present in that crusade—the growth of the crowd, for example. The first night we may have had 5,000 people scattered around that coliseum. But after the healings and testimonies, the second night crowd grew to 8,000. The third night the place was packed with 10,000 or more jammed inside. And by the last night, police estimates said that almost 10,000 were turned away. There was just no room. In some areas of the building, the people were so crowded that it was impossible to sit down. All the corridors and aisles were packed with people. If we had stayed, we would have gone outside, and the audience would have grown to 50,000.

This was because of the healings?

That's right. The pastors and the radio advertising had gone on for weeks. The local churches had promoted it. In Roxas City, for example, the Assemblies of God congregation had made an extraordinary effort, with many other churches helping. But after the first night, the crowd will only build if something happens. All that work had brought out 5,000 people. What happened was that first night brought out the rest. It all happens by word of mouth.

By the last night the doctors were starting to bring their patients out of their hospital beds. In fact, some of them were still in their beds with their IVs still hooked up. The provincial governor's brother was brought out in a wheelchair. Doctors and nurses were all over the place with special cases of terminally ill people. It looked tragic and pitiful. There were twisted bodies with grotesque cancers hanging from them.

The doctors were delighted, which surprised me. I saw one who was very earnestly interviewing one of the people who had just claimed a healing. I wrongly assumed that the person was complaining that she really wasn't healed after all. But the doctor smiled, "Oh no, this is one of my patients, and she can now hear perfectly out of this deaf ear. This really happened."

I've seen that over and over. The bridge between medicine and faith is not as far as we assume. Of course, I have no power. God is the one who is doing everything. But doctors also know how limited they really are. They know that medicine only helps speed up the natural healing process. And then, in their daily practice, they see how powerfully faith works. When they speak with authority and assurance, it can have quite an effect on a patient. "It will go away in three days." All kinds of studies are made to show how some people improve even though the medicine is in fact a placebo, not really a medicine at all.

Doctors understand the natural world. It is not such a great leap to the supernatural. After all, the *supernatural* is just what the word implies; it is *super* natural. It is not unnatural. It is the healing process speeded up by the power of God. If the doctor is a Christian, he will see these events as miracles of God. If he is not a Christian, he will attribute it to suggestion or something else, but very few doctors still argue that nothing is happening. When they come to a meeting, some are surprised at how comfortable they feel when they always assumed that they would be hostile.

By the last night it seemed as if every sick or handicapped person in the city had come out. Isn't that overwhelming? And so many of these are not healed. It is so sad to see them struggling to walk or trying to believe. Are you giving them false hope?

I'm overwhelmed by the people who are healed. I'm thanking God for that.

Sure, if you focus on those who aren't healed, it can break your heart. Yes, it's sad. But it is also inspiring. They are trying. Again and again, we are told that people who are handicapped need to be challenged and not smothered with sympathy. They need to make an effort. But our instinct is to protect them.

Let me tell you something that is even more sad than seeing these people who are not healed. That is the person who may not really be crippled at all. He or she just needs a moment of faith, a trigger, a point of contact that will get him or her going. But the person just doesn't know it. Many people may live their lives as a cripple or as a beggar in rags on a street in a big Asian city, never knowing that they are only a single moment away from a miracle. That is sad.

Why doesn't God heal everybody?

Of course, I don't know the answer to that question. Nobody does. There are some who theorize that it is all in the hands of the person who wants the healing. However, God has set certain laws in the universe, and they must act on them. It is in their hands. Their faith will bring the answer. Others say that it is all God's sovereign decision. Others believe that some are given gifts to heal, although that viewpoint has been in disfavor in recent years. There are Scriptures to defend each of those concepts, and there is probably some truth in them all.

That same question is asked in various forms all through the Bible, and it is just not answered. There must be a reason. Yet God seems to purposely ignore it. On one such occasion the disciples asked, "Why was this man born blind? Did he sin or his parents sin?"

Jesus had the perfect opportunity to give an explanation about why some things happen to one person and not to another. Instead, His answer provoked dozens of more questions. Jesus said, "It wasn't because of his sins or his parent's sins. He was born blind so that I can heal him."

Gideon asked the angel the question, "If God is with us, why have the Midianites oppressed Israel these past seven years?" This was a good question, a reasonable question. One could just as well ask, "If God is with us, why am I going through this divorce? Why is my baby sick? Why do orphans die on the streets of Calcutta?"

This was a perfect chance for God to explain why He allows human suffering. But the angel didn't give Gideon any kind of an explanation. He ignored the question and responded with a command. "Go in your power and save your country."

That's very typical of God. The Bible is full of such encounters.

Question. "Why do orphans die on the streets of Calcutta?"

God's answer? "Feed them."

"If God loves me, then why am I sick?"

God's answer? "Be healed."

"If there is a loving God, why did He allow my mother to die of cancer?"

God's answer? "Find the cure to cancer."

Apparently God doesn't want to cry over spilled milk. For some reason He won't respond to that particular question. Maybe we wouldn't understand His answer. Why had Israel suffered under the Midianites for seven years? The angel ignored the question. His message was that now Israel was going to be delivered.

When I go into a healing crusade, I don't have answers for why those people have been going through a crisis or why they are suffering. I come with deliverance in Jesus' name.

You've been in this healing business for years now. You've seen all the great ministries and made a lifetime study of them. What have you learned? What have you concluded?

This is my fortieth year of ministry, and there is still so much that I don't know or understand.

One of the few conclusions I've come to is the importance of a point of contact. All through Scriptures it is there. When there is a miracle, there is a point of contact. Of course, there is the Scripture that says, "These signs shall follow them that believe...they shall lay hands on the sick, and they shall recover" (Mk. 16:17-18).

In the Book of James it says, "Is any sick among you? let him call for the elders of the church; and let them pray over him, anointing him with oil in the name of the Lord: and the prayer of faith shall save the sick, and the Lord shall raise him up; and if he have committed sins, they shall be forgiven him" (Jas. 5:14-15).

There are so many other examples of points of contact, and they are all so diverse. The woman touched the hem of Jesus' garment, and she was healed. Naaman the leper dipped in the Jordan River to receive his healing. Peter's shadow brought healing as he passed by people in the streets. According to Acts 19:11-12, the apostle Paul prayed over cloths. These cloths were laid on the sick, and the sick recovered. Oil is often used as a point of contact.

You get some criticism for that. Some say that you are marketing prayer cloths or vials of oil.

I'm sensitive to that criticism. But I'm willing to live with it because of the results. We never charge money for such an item. They are given to anyone who calls our office or writes for one. But I sincerely believe in such a practice. My mother tells the story of how she had complications during my birth and how a man walked into the county hospital and placed an anointed handkerchief on her head. She said that a light filled the room, and she was healed. The first miracle I saw involved the use of oil. I can't tell you how many testimonies we receive.

I'm told that we just got a letter in about a child who fell from a third story window. Apparently, the child was dead. But when they laid the cloth on the child, he started breathing again. I do know that the Bible says in First Corinthians 1:27, "But God hath chosen the foolish things of the world to confound the wise; and God hath chosen the weak things of the world to confound the things which are mighty."

Let me tell you a story about a woman who was healed of deafness in Nigeria. God taught me a wonderful lesson from the experience. This was in the 1970's. The crowds were huge. The first night of the crusade I preached from John 9:6, where Jesus spit on the ground, made mud, and put in on the blind man's eyes. He told him to go wash in the pool of Siloam, and when the blind man obeyed he was healed. The idea was, if you obey the Word of God in this crusade, God will touch you.

When I came off the platform that night there was a huge crowd. Security guards were rushing me to my car, but a very big African man stood in the way. He must have been close to seven feet tall. And he must have weighed 300 pounds. Somehow his faith had been inspired by the sermon, and he passed me a note. When I got to my hotel room I read it. "My wife is deaf," it said. "But when you spit in her ears she will be healed."

There was no way that I was going to spit in his wife's ears. My American cultural background would not allow me to do it. I have great respect for black people, and the spectacle of a white man spitting in the ears of a black woman revolted me.

Every night for five nights, he pushed his way through our security and handed me a similar note. On the last day of the crusade, as I was leaving the platform, he once more broke through our security and this time he grabbed me. He literally lifted me off my feet, looked me in the eyes, and said, "You are going to spit in my wife's ears, and you are going to do it now!"

Well, I was exhausted and even a bit angry. So I decided, *Okay, bring her on. I'll spit in her ears*. To my amazement, she was healed. Right then, I got down on my knees to ask God for forgiveness. Now, the man was Moslem, but God had spoken to him and told him what the point of contact should be. He and his wife believed it. It was their faith that had healed them. Of course, he converted to Christianity. To this day he preaches all over Nigeria.

But there it is again, a point of contact. The woman with the issue of blood knew that she would be healed if she could touch the hem of Jesus' garment. The people knew that they would be healed when Peter's shadow passed over their bodies.

What kind of follow-up is there in these large crusades? What happens to all these people afterward?

The local churches follow up. In Roxas City, the large Assemblies of God congregation will help spearhead the follow-up effort. In much of the Philippines, the Miracle Life Fellowship, which was founded by my ministry, will do the follow-up.

Tell me about Miracle Life Fellowship. For all practical purposes, it is a denomination, is it not?

I like to think of it as a fellowship, but I suppose that every movement moves that way. Government agencies force it to happen.

How many churches are a part of Miracle Life Fellowship?

In the Philippines there are more than 300 churches. In that regard, it is almost the size of the Assemblies of God in that country. It is much bigger than a lot of traditional Protestant denominations.

How did that happen? A.A. Allen preached against denominations for years, yet now his successor builds a denomination of his own.

A.A. Allen conducted many crusades in the Philippines. He had actually started a Bible school there. All I can say is that God really gave me a burden for missions. So when I took over the ministry, I started spending more and more time in South America, Africa, and Asia. Each year we were pouring more money into the Philippines work. I just fell in love with the people.

The key to our success in the Philippines was to take the gospel to the poor. We felt that this was our scriptural mandate. Our Filipino students started opening churches in places that had never heard the gospel. We went into the center of headhunter country, for example. Now that was really "pioneer" work in the truest sense of the word. We didn't just feed the people spiritually. We fed them physically. But it all paid off. There was a tremendous harvest of souls.

Many of our Filipino converts went on to become pastors and evangelists, and they remained affiliated with our ministry. Let me give you a good example. Dario Bautista is the pastor of a growing church in Canlubang, Laguna, Philippines. But the steps that led him to active involvement in ministry are reflective of how our ministry has influenced church growth in many places.

Bautista was raised in a very large family, with 12 brothers and sisters. He was rebellious and constantly in trouble. One day he had a fight with one of his brothers, and he wound up stabbing his brother pretty seriously. Knowing he was in big trouble, he dashed outside the house and ran right into a barbed wire fence. Along with assorted cuts and lacerations, he lost the sight in one of his eyes.

Years passed, and eventually Bautista got saved in a local church. When I came to Manila for a crusade at Araneta Coliseum in 1979, his pastor asked him to attend the crusade and believe for a miracle of healing. He didn't know what I was preaching because he didn't understand English. But Bautista could feel and see what God was doing for other people with all kinds of diseases, and his faith began to soar. When he left the service that night, he felt something like a flicker in his eye. In a few days he could see light. It was a few days later when his sight was completely restored.

Bautista felt a strong call to the ministry, so he enrolled in Miracle Life Bible College and finished the Pastoral Ministry Course in 1987.

A year later, he affiliated with our Miracle Life Fellowship in the Philippines. Today, of course, his church is one of the fastest growing congregations in Canlubang. Pastor Dario recently donated a 2,000 square meter lot to my ministry. In honor of A.A. Allen, the man who started it all, I have named the acreage Miracle Valley.

This gives you an idea of how our church fellowship has grown in the Philippines through the years.

Worldwide, how many churches have you launched?

Worldwide? Either directly or indirectly, very close to 1,000 churches. Beyond that, there have been numerous clinics, orphanages, and schools.

Sometimes these works are on the cutting edge of evangelism, located in places that most big denominations or ministries would never go. Because of that we sometimes pay a price. In Liberia, for example, we had six feeding centers. There are 12 schools with 2,700 students, four health centers, and the only residential school for the deaf in the country. We were in the villages building wells, putting in sewage facilities, and providing nutritional guidance. Then the civil war hit. Some of the work was wiped out. Many of our pastors had to flee the country. Others had to pick up the pieces and start over.

Have you made a transition from the large evangelistic crusades to famine relief and feeding programs?

I still do both. Feed My People is the name of our humanitarian work, and we do relief development and community development benefiting churches and cities all over the world. We even have an outreach in the United States to Native Americans. Former speaker of the House, Newt Gingrich, visited our Food Bank while he held that position, and he called it an example of an effective charity. It was a big, front-page story. We received the "President's Award" from the National Charities Award Committee for outstanding humanitarian service. Former President Reagan was the keynote speaker. But the Don Stewart Ministries are still going strong. We sponsor meetings all over the world. I still go to many of the so-called Third World nations, and there is a crusade each year in the United Kingdom.

For years, I conducted massive crusades. We had some of the largest crusades in the history of Brazil, El Salvador, Guatemala, the Philippines, and many African countries. In Manila, the Philippine newspapers estimated the crowds at 500,000. Only the Pope and Billy Graham later drew bigger audiences.

You saw what was happening in Korononadahl? If we had moved outside, we would have soon been drawing 50,000, and it would have kept going. And yet, we have found that the follow-up in such a mammoth crusade is beyond proper management. We found that a smaller crusade, with well-planned follow-up, can be more effective in the long run. But we learned that the most effective follow-up of all is the establishment of new churches. So, we began to adapt to what we had learned, and we built churches. I think that it has been more effective. But there is a place for both.

I've seen pictures of you with President Ford, President Reagan, and every Philippine president of your lifetime—Marcos, Aquino, and Ramos—as well as former President Duarte of El Salvador. You have pictures of many African heads of state. From John Dowie down to the present, political leaders seem to have this strange fascination for evangelists. I saw it in your meeting with the governor during your Philippine crusade.

I think it stems from the large crowds. When you draw audiences over 100,000, you are pretty hard to miss. The first ones to look you over are the politicians. Then there is the mystique and charisma that surrounds the miracles that become greater with each retelling. By the time they get back to the presidential palace, they must be quite exaggerated.

You know there is a different story to each of those photos. In one of our Philippine crusades, a prominent member of Marcos' staff was visiting, and he looked up and saw a woman's goiter disappear with his own eyes. He saw it just collapse. Well, he converted to Christ and soon became my chief advocate in the halls of power. We went on television in that country and met many people, including President and Mrs. Marcos, who often asked for my prayers, and later, Cory Aquino and General Ramos.

In El Salvador, I prayed for President Duarte. The country was in great turmoil. The civil war was at its peak. I was preaching in a bulletproof vest. I expected the meeting to last for 15 minutes, but he poured his heart out to me for almost three hours.

Why don't you have such big crusades in the United States?

When I first took the reins from A.A. Allen back in 1970, I planned a large crusade in New York City's Madison Square Garden. I was told that it had not been filled for a healing crusade since John Dowie, and that was the old Garden. Well, we filled it. It was a great moment. The religious and secular publications made a big deal out of it, which was personally satisfying. It was splashed across the country by the *Associated Press*, and even *Rolling Stone* magazine carried it. But eventually, I came away from that experience with a renewed zeal for missions. For the same amount of money, one can do so much more in other countries. There are already many ministers in the United States. My burden, my concern, slowly shifted to the poor and suffering people of South America, Africa, and Asia. We called it a *Compassion Explosion*. We decided to move out of our comfort zone and to take the gospel to a hurting world. There is so much need in those countries and so little help.

Ironically, one needs an American presence to help finance a ministry in such foreign countries. So in the past year I have started to rebuild my American ministry. We have just begun a nationwide television ministry as well in key cities. One of my decisions to work on this book with you was born out of a desire to rebuild a stateside ministry.

Where did it all begin for you? How did you suddenly wake up as a healing evangelist?

I can identify with most of the stories of other such evangelists since my own is so similar. My family was very poor. We lived in a small, dirty, Arizona desert town, a mining community. In those days, there was a part of town for the poor Mexican Americans and a part of town for the Anglos. They even had separate public swimming pools, which I suppose sounds extravagant to some, but in Arizona where temperatures never fall below 100 all summer long, a public swimming pool is almost a life-and-death requirement. Well, we lived with the Mexican Americans. I felt more comfortable swimming with them than with the Anglos.

I remember my mother and father praying for food and someone giving us charity by leaving sacks of food on our doorstep to help us. We were really poor.

A goat provided milk for the family. In fact, my first example of answered prayer involved that old goat. Somehow it had gotten into some poison and had eaten it. Well, that goat started foaming at the mouth, and it finally fell over, apparently dead. My Dad and Mom knelt down beside it and prayed. They even anointed it with oil. "You know, God, that we depend on this goat for our milk. We can't feed this little family of six children without it. You just can't let him die." The goat hopped up on its feet and that was that.

Just as in the story of so many of these evangelists, I had my own personal healing. At 12 years of age I was struck with a degenerative bone disease. Within a matter of months, I was a cripple. It was a bitter time for me. My classmates ridiculed me. I felt like God had abandoned me. I rebelled against my parents' faith. *What did they know? What had God done for them? Look how poor they were.*

Because we were Pentecostals, the kids at school called us "holy rollers." So it was a triple blow. I was ridiculed because of my poverty, because of my faith, and because of my handicap. I was a pretty miserable fellow.

But in my heart, I knew all along that God was real and that my parents, poor as they may be, had a peace that most people would never have. Sometimes I would tune in to A.A. Allen on the radio at night and I would hear the prayer for the sick, and I would hear God's whisper that He was not my enemy; He was my friend and He would heal me if I had faith. One night our church showed Oral Roberts' new movie, *Venture Into Faith*, and all through the movie my spirit cried out to God to heal me and to take away the shame and ridicule of being a cripple.

In 1952, still on crutches, I stumbled into a tiny Assemblies of God church in Cottonwood, Arizona. A country preacher prayed for me, and that night I walked out of the church on my own two feet. I stood there looking up into the stars praising God. I was gloriously saved and healed. Afterward, I joined up with the Allen ministry, driving trucks and putting up his tent. Eventually I began to minister in the meetings.

Just like that?

Well, there was a transition. I was still a teenager. I was in and out of trouble during those years. I went to Canyonville Bible Academy, a Christian boarding school in Oregon. In my senior year, I was kicked out. Then one night I heard on the radio that A.A. Allen was going to be in Phoenix, Arizona, so I went down to take a look. When I walked into that tent and felt the power of God, I said to myself, *I don't ever want to leave this.* I renewed my commitment to the Lord, and the next day, I went up to one of the staff. "I'll help out, do anything you want," I said. "I'll work all day just for food." As it turned out, they had just lost a truck driver, so they took me on the spot. And I got paid.

Allen had many associated ministers?

Yes. That was very unusual. Some of the big ministers fostered the idea of "I'm God's vessel and you aren't." In contrast to such arrogance,

Allen encouraged and helped nurture young ministers, men and women, black and white, to follow him into ministries of their own. And he shared his platform with them.

One of the greatest of these was R.W. Shambach. He was a powerful preacher and still is. I was in awe of his preaching technique, his rhythm, and his sense of the dramatic. I suppose, if he had launched out on his own a little later and had thus been closer to the Allen ministry at the time of Allen's death, he would have very likely taken it over. It is really wonderful to see a new generation enjoy his powerful preaching through the Trinity Broadcasting Network.

What was the relationship between A.A. Allen and these younger men?

Oh, he was like a father. He was wonderful. He was full of enthusiasm and ideas for them. There was never a hint of any jealousy or fear. His own ministry was very strong. Only shortly before his death did he betray any insecurity when he made a comment to me that maybe he wasn't needed anymore. But this is a feeling that comes to all of us at that age and time in our lives.

Was there a power struggle after his death?

There was none immediately. The ministry needed money to keep afloat. We were a million dollars in debt. The board knew that Allen had handpicked me and discipled me to be his successor, and they knew that they needed someone strong. So they were unanimous that I should lead it. They all understood that the leader had to be strong, in the A.A. Allen tradition. The people were not going to follow someone unless they thought that he was really in charge and was being led and directed by the Holy Spirit. They needed someone who was hearing from God. But in their hearts, some of the board may have felt that because I was young—I was only 30 at the time—that I could be controlled and would serve as a figurehead while they ran things.

Understand, these were not naive people. They had been with A.A. Allen through denominational fights and legal hassles. Allen had been persecuted by local and state governments. They knew the business side of such a ministry—where its money comes from, where it goes. They also knew that the man on the platform, the person put out front, would soon have the following, and thus, the power. What they had in mind was not going to be easy.

With the experience I have now, I may have handled things much differently. In some situations maybe I should have been stronger and in others much more gentle and patient.

We had over 200 employees at the time in Miracle Valley. The ministry was in the process of a transition into computers. Many of the employees were not skilled in this area. I had to lay off over 100 people at one time to enable the ministry to survive. This was traumatic for me. These people had families. They were all living at Miracle Valley. At the time, there were no other jobs available. So this was one of the hardest things that I had ever done. I couldn't sleep at night. Many times I would walk the floor and cry out to God for help.

Every time I turned around, someone was taking a verbal shot at me. Some thought that I was trying to be too much like Allen. I had been under his ministry for years, so I did have many of his pulpit mannerisms and phrases. Other people who had been touched by Allen's ministry thought that I was moving too far away from his memory. Some thought I was too close to the Assemblies of God and other denominations. The general superintendent of the Assemblies of God at that time, Thomas Zimmerman, had taken a liking to me, and we had begun to fellowship together. Of course, the Assemblies had their eye on our growing fellowship of churches in the Philippines and wanted us to merge with them.

Some wanted me to get up and publically defend A.A. Allen from all the accusations surrounding his death. They thought I was being disrespectful and ungrateful for not speaking out more. But then, they didn't know what really happened, and I wasn't going to lie about it.

Eventually, some of the staff and board tried to take over the ministry. They brought forth all kinds of accusations that sounded very serious—that is, until given an explanation. Well, their attempt failed, so they went to the local government. They knew very well the local government bias against independent, Pentecostal ministries. After all, they had lived with it for years. They knew just what buttons to push and what allegations to make and what records to show. Worst of all, they themselves were responsible for recording and keeping some of the documentation that they were now using as "evidence." I had no idea if they had falsified something or failed to keep an important receipt or purposely used the incorrect legal language on a document or recorded minutes.

It was a very difficult time for me. I had to essentially give it all over to the Lord. I resolved that if this was what He wanted, if He wanted the ministry brought down like this, I couldn't do anything about it.

There were big, front-page headlines with all kinds of charges. But in the end, I had to conclude that it was a wonderful experience. We were clean. None of the charges held up. Thankfully, we could document everything. There was a very important added bonus from the experience; we came away with an even greater understanding of the dangerous relationship between church and state. We were able to put in place very strict, absolute policies to help guide us into the future when ministries would receive even greater scrutiny and control by government.

Chapter Nine

Transition to the Charismatic Renewal

Kathryn Kuhlman

Your ministry started just as the healing revival of the 1950's was coming to an end, at least in the United States and most of the English-speaking world. Were people aware of the transition that was taking place? Could you sense that things were changing?

Oh, without question. The charismatic movement had begun in the historic churches. In 1960, Dennis Bennett, an Episcopal priest from California, claimed he had experienced the "gift of tongues"; that is, speaking a language he hadn't learned. He was openly praying for the sick in his church. In the 1940's and 50's this would have been considered heresy. Two years later the United Presbyterian Church officially decided that the "charismatic gifts" were "valid for believers today." Then one by one all the mainline churches slowly began to open their doors, including the Catholics, who experienced perhaps the biggest revival of all beginning in the late 1960's, growing to involve millions of believers, including a number of bishops, Cardinal Suenens, and others. The only holdouts were the Fundamentalists who, in the tradition of religious critics of New Testament times, insisted that if there were miracles, they were of the devil.

I might add, within time there was a third group, which no one has really written about or explained: the classical Pentecostals, often independents, who were themselves a bit uncomfortable with some of their own cultural baggage. They decided they wanted to be "charismatics" too, so they frequented Catholic prayer groups or simply started calling themselves charismatics. Eventually these vast numbers co-opted the charismatic movement or simply drove most of the inquiring traditional Christians right back into their denominations. Today, outside of the prayer groups within the Catholic church that are no longer ecumenical, most so-called "charismatics" are now just plain independent Pentecostals with a fancier name.

Your own ministry must have changed during this period.

My own ministry was in turmoil. I was an anachronism. I had people advising me to quit shouting when I preached, to sit on a stool on the platform and just teach the people. Others wanted me to declare that the new charismatics were of the devil and to be more fiery than ever. Now, keep in mind. I had just taken the reins of the biggest, active ministry of its kind in the world. Oral Roberts had long since left the sawdust trail. We had several hundred employees, and as I explained, a one million dollar debt. That's the equivalent of six million in 1990's dollars. Then there was the first of several takeover attempts to drive me out of my own organization. This was not a time for an identity crisis.

Of course, all of this drove me to my knees, and with God's help we survived the transition. According to many observers, this ministry is the one, truest link to the healing revival of the 1940's and 50's, still functioning according to its original purpose.

One of the old healing evangelists experienced a tremendous boon to his ministries. Kenneth Hagin, who had been around for years, with very little to show for it, was suddenly filling auditoriums and seeing his books and tapes sell by the thousands. Hagin became the father of the *Word of Faith movement*, and many others followed, such as Kenneth and Gloria Copeland, Fred Price, Marilyn Hickey, Robert Tilton, and others.

Of all the "Word of Faith" ministers, who would you consider the forerunner today?

By far, Kenneth and Gloria Copeland are at the top of the list. Their "Believer's Voice of Victory" is still teaching the uncompromising message throughout the world. They have become the leading contemporary voice in this area and have influenced the lives of many today who are continuing the message, such as Creflo Dollar.

Some made the transition to the charismatic renewal and some didn't?

That's exactly right.

There was a vast cultural chasm between old-line, denominational Pentecostals and the new charismatics from the traditional Christian churches. Pentecostalism had been born in rural America and was greatly influenced by black culture, especially in its music. A minister wasn't considered "anointed" if he didn't shout, breathlessly and loudly, from the pulpit. Ministries like Kenneth Hagin's, which had been more low key, had gone unappreciated. Now, they were suddenly "discovered" by the new charismatic Christians who were hungry for the theology of faith and healing and the other gifts of the Holy Spirit, but turned off by the peculiar style of most Pentecostal preachers.

In fact, the term *charismatic*, which comes from the Greek word *charisma*, meaning "gift," was a way for the new Pentecostals to define themselves apart from the old-line or "classical" Pentecostals. The two groups shared the same theology but little else.

So you survived the transition and moved on with the addition of Feed My People?

That's right. That was the one thing to come out of the struggle. More and more I realized that God had blessed A.A. Allen's ministry because he had taken his message to the poor. It was not operated as a business, as are many ministries of today. This was missions. And more and more, I felt that this was to be my own calling, even more so than it had been under Allen. So *Feed My People* was born. We took care of the poor and God took care of us.

Then, there was that nagging question of my ministerial style. I really needed to feel free to follow the leading of the Holy Spirit. That may mean going from worship right into the operation of the gifts of the Spirit. It may mean preaching right in the middle of the song service. I didn't work very well in a structured environment. So, out of necessity, I took the ministry overseas where I could be myself.

What was the timing on all of this? How quickly was the transition made to missions, for example?

A.A. Allen died in 1970. We carried the television program for another two years and radio until 1974. But by 1976, our ministry was pretty much overseas. With no regrets, by the way. This was how God was leading me, and it was a very real and logical extension of Allen's ministry to the poor, which was the work of Jesus.

And yet some continued here in the United States and thrived during the charismatic renewal. Some, but not very many. I mentioned Kenneth Hagin. There were a few others. But the new charismatic evangelists had a different lifestyle. Bob Mumford, Derek Prince, Don Basham—these were men with writing ministries that had wide appeal, and yet they prayed for the sick and saw great miracles. A number of Catholic evangelists emerged. But the greatest during this time had to be Kathryn Kuhlman.

Where had she been all this time?

For years, she had been ministering to crowds in Pittsburgh, Pennsylvania, and nearby Youngstown, Ohio. There had been some wonderful miracles, and as a result, she had a very loyal audience. The fact that she had avoided contact with the *Voice of Healing* enabled her to escape some of the extremes that were later associated with some of those ministries. As a result, her audience included many Catholics and denominational people. All of that increased as the charismatic movement took hold. In fact, the first Catholic Pentecostal retreat took place near Pittsburgh, and there was soon a large group in Youngstown.

Kathryn's real entrance to the charismatic world came through the Full Gospel Business Men International. We really haven't talked much about this group. But this was an organization founded by Demos Shakarian and was basically a group of donors and supporters of Oral Roberts. In fact, Roberts gets very little credit for the role he played in encouraging this organization to get going. These were the same people who helped promote Tommy Hicks, who had conducted the historic crusade in Argentina. They also gave a platform to Bill Branham in his later years.

Most Catholic histories of the charismatic movement in their church downplay the role of these businessmen. It's important for Catholics to authenticate what happened within a Catholic context. But the Full Gospel Business Men were right in the thick of it and became a common meeting place for traditional Pentecostals and their newer charismatic cousins. Kathryn Kuhlman became an instant celebrity with this crowd.

What was the appeal? In some ways she was much more mystical and dramatic than any of the other healing evangelists.

She was dramatic, but not loud or breathless. She didn't rant. And being mystical was not a problem for Catholics. Their history was full of mystics. Being a woman wasn't a problem either. Kathryn could speak their language, and that was an important part of her appeal. After ministering to non-Pentecostals for years, she knew some of the little things to say to reassure the various denominational people in her audience. She wouldn't allow any public manifestations of the gifts of the Spirit, which offended many visiting Pentecostals, but moderated her image and guaranteed that there would be no fanatical outbursts. This was a healing service that a Presbyterian could come to. In fact, right in the middle of the charismatic renewal, she was invited to hold weekly services at Bob Lamont's First Presbyterian Church in downtown Pittsburgh.

This was the moment for which Kathryn Kuhlman was born. Her personal marriage troubles of youth, which had driven her into isolation and work with denominational people, now served a purpose. Her life experiences were suddenly integrated. She had lived to see God's purpose or use for it all.

Remember, the big thing, always, in any of these stories, are the miracles themselves. The secret to the Branham phenomenon, for example, was the healings—not his personality or his teaching. When the miracles stopped, Branham kept right on going; but the phenomenon had ended. And so it was with Kathryn Kuhlman. The key to her emergence in the 1960's and 70's was the long list of miraculous healings, documented and publicly recorded.

She was a hit. Her television program had the highest ratings for religious programming. She was invited onto the Johnny Carson Show. Incidentally, Johnny asked her if it wasn't true that most of the healings were psychosomatic? In essence, she replied, "So what?" Her monthly visits to the Shrine Mosque in Los Angeles had crowds lined up hours in advance. Chartered buses came from Vancouver, Canada. She took one national tour after another and packed out auditoriums everywhere.

Earlier, you talked about a turning point in Franklin, Pennsylvania, when everything changed.

Yes, a lady was healed. And the miracle happened while Kathryn was preaching, even without the laying on of hands. When Kathryn heard about it, she started encouraging all her audiences to reach out and take their healing without waiting for her. And soon it began to happen. Perhaps Kathryn felt that there was something egotistical about someone laying hands on another person, as if to say, "Now that I touch you, you can be healed." This new phenomenon fit her style and her emphasis that no man or woman can heal, it is only and always God. She would always say, "God healed you, not Kathryn Kuhlman."

What do you think?

I totally agree with her. Of course, only God can heal. I like the style too. We have all learned from her and we all use some of her formula, some even to the point of her exact words and actions. But personally, I want to be yielded to God so that He can use me in any of the gifts of the Spirit, including discerning of spirits, word of knowledge, and prophecy. I also believe in the laying on of hands. The Bible encourages it. Believe me, it is not egotistical; it is a humbling experience. I continue to practice it out of obedience to the Word. It isn't the only way, but it is one very scriptural way. As I see it, God uses different personalities and styles to reach different people. Kathryn Kuhlman's appeal within traditional Christianity seemed to open the doors to a wider secular following.

Some credit that to a *Redbook* magazine article in the 1950's. It was an investigation piece with a whole team of reporters fanning out across the country to do what they assumed would be an exposé. But when they stumbled onto some verifiable examples of actual healings, their whole project changed. By the time they had finished they had found a variety of unexplained "miracles" that seemed to defy every explanation a skeptic could offer. Of course, the magazine was braced for ridicule and controversy so they made sure they had all their facts, X-rays, Workman's Compensation reports, and doctors lined up. When the article hit it was of only passing interest to Pentecostals, who knew all along that God healed the sick, but it was a real shocker to some in traditional Christianity and the secular world.

The *Redbook* experience must have affirmed for Kathryn Kuhlman the power of validating an answer to prayer and documenting everything that had happened. Her books of documented miracles became bestsellers to a wide audience of American readers, which created an even wider circle of believers. Twenty years later, in 1970, *Time* magazine called her a "one woman shrine of Lourdes," making the remarkable acknowledgment that "healings seem to be happening."

And these people who were healed are still around?

They're still out there. Wayne Warner, who is perhaps the leading authority on the history of the Pentecostal movement, wrote an excellent biography on Kuhlman, going directly to many of the people who had claimed healing in her ministry. Many of them outlived Kathryn herself.

I remember hearing the testimony of a Houston police captain, John LeVrier. John was a Baptist who didn't especially believe in healing. Then he was told that he had prostate cancer. It had spread throughout his body, and he was now too far gone to do anything about it. He went to Kuhlman's meeting at the Shriner's Auditorium in Los Angeles. Miss Kuhlman pointed up to him in the balcony and said, "There is someone being healed of cancer up there. Stand up and take your healing."

He stood and felt a warm sensation throughout his body. When he got back to Houston he announced his healing to his family and declared that he no longer needed his medicine. This, of course, alarmed some of his friends and aroused his doctor to action. But extensive X-rays showed that the cancer was indeed gone. Nothing was there. Someone published a book about it, and LeVrier told his story at Full Gospel Business Men's meetings across the country. There were thousands of these type of stories, dozens of them made into books and tracts.

Toward the end of her ministry, auditoriums were packed with the terminally ill. You commented about how the sick started pouring out of the hospitals the last few days of my crusade in Korononadahl. They had heard about the miracles that had happened earlier in the week. Well, just imagine what it would be like if there were healing services there every month for decades? Kathryn kept going to Youngstown and Los Angeles, and she kept her regular services in Pittsburgh. It drew huge crowds of desperate people.

How did she deal with that? Obviously, not everyone was healed. In fact, as in the case of most evangelists, the vast majority were not healed. How did her theology evolve over the years?

Her theology and her style went through several transitions. In the earlier years she urged her new converts to get out of the churches that didn't emphasize being born again and didn't allow for a belief that God could heal the sick. In latter years, she encouraged people to stay where they were to be an influence for good. And as to the phenomenon of "falling under the power," there was none of that in Denver or even Franklin. It slowly started happening in Pittsburgh and soon became a staple in her services. In many respects this phenomenon helped sensationalize her meetings and draw the bigger crowds that came in the 1970's.

As to her views on healing, if one accepts what she said from the pulpit, she became increasingly impressed with the sovereignty of God. The faith of the believer was a part of it, but God really made that decision and one might as well relax and see what He was going to do.

Where does Kathryn Kuhlman fit in the whole history of this movement? How does one summarize her ministry?

Some fault her for not leaving behind an organization that could continue. This is the success of Oral Roberts. In fact, Oral is famous for the quote, "There is no success without a successor." It is what A.A. Allen did with me. But in so many ways, she was the best of them all. Her finances were impeccable at a time when many ministries were in trouble for cutting corners or just poor management. She was generous, a giver to hundreds of causes and charities. Much of it was unknown until after her death, which makes it even more impressive. She had begrudging acceptance from a very skeptical, secular world. In that, she was almost alone. She was humble, always, carefully directing the glory to God.

You know, interestingly enough, her ministry practically spanned the whole time period of the great healing revival. She started out by traveling with her sister and brother-in-law, an evangelistic team that had been inspired by Dr. Charles Price.

Later, she was briefly a student at Aimee Semple McPherson's school in Los Angeles, so she saw "Sister" preach. When the William Branham phenomenon hit, she and some of her staff snuck into a Branham meeting, coming away admitting that this was really a work of God. In her latter years, she became a friend of Oral Roberts. ORU gave her an honorary doctorate, and she had Richard Roberts singing in her crusades.

For a while, some thought that the whole healing revival had died with Kathryn Kuhlman. In the United States, there was a huge, huge vacuum after she passed. In many respects, she is the most attractive or the most "classy" of the great healing evangelists. And by the way, she would never consider herself a "healing evangelist." She was just an "evangelist." She preached that the greatest miracle was being born again. The healings that happened were God's business.

Chapter Ten

From the Present to the Future

Benny Hinn and the Future

Perhaps no one has had a better ringside seat for viewing this revival than yourself. What are your conclusions? What happened?

The healing ministry was restored to the Church, to where it belongs. That's the bottom line. Sure, there were mistakes made by all of us. There were sometimes extremes of doctrine. There were evangelists who became arrogant or proud. A few may have been insincere. Although in my experience, most were very sincere people. Yet, God used it for His purposes.

And it's over?

Yes. It's over, at least in the sense that the Azusa Street Revival is over. I know that such a comment will make some very angry. They think that things should always get better and better, and they superstitiously believe that one is in danger of making a self-fulfilling prophecy by saying out loud that a revival has come and gone. Yet it's true.

Now, this doesn't mean that the ministry of healing has gone. It has stayed, and it is practiced today with more dignity and perhaps in a way more in keeping with the traditions of the Church than it was in the heydays of the 1950's. There may even be more healings today than there were in the height of the revival, which might also explain why it isn't such a big deal. A 1996 cover story for *Time* magazine practically concludes that faith healings are a fact. Of course, the article doesn't recognize any of the scriptural absolutes that we hold dear. It lumps New Age "miracles" in with all the rest. But it does demonstrate how far we have come from the days when A.A. Allen was harassed and sometimes arrested for preaching his message. It is one more demonstration of the fact that there is an innate hunger for the supernatural. If the Church won't step up and assume its role, spiritualists, mediums, and New Agers will.

You say that it's over and yet the Benny Hinn meetings are bigger than ever. Auditoriums are packed across the country with thousands waiting outside.

That's right, and he is the exception that proves the rule. As we've stated before, there will continue to be that slender thread. Benny Hinn will be followed by someone else. It will go on and on, and it may even break out in another explosion. But we have returned to that time when there is only one great healing evangelist in this country—a John Dowie followed by an Aimee Semple McPherson followed by a Charles Price. There are not 200 such evangelists, or even 50. There is Benny Hinn, no one else. In the world beyond America, there is Morris Cerullo, whose first priority must of necessity be his *Inspirational Television Network*. There are also Reinhard Bonnke and myself. As of this writing, these four are the only large ongoing healing ministries still conducting crusades.

How does Benny Hinn compare to the others?

In many ways, he is the beneficiary of all the ministries that have gone on before. He has inculcated parts and pieces of all of them while still being himself. Of course, his quite open admiration of Kathryn Kuhlman is apparent. It is pretty hard to miss her influence, not only in the healing services, but in the preaching as well.

Does that diminish him somewhat?

Not at all. Now, it would if he were not so open about it. If he were to pretend that everything was uniquely his idea, then it would backfire on him. He would appear presumptive. But his very public admiration for Kathryn Kuhlman's style and ministry is actually rather charming and a humble thing for him to do.

We talked before about the little rituals and techniques that evangelists come to rely on, the formula, if you will. Are these evident in a Benny Hinn crusade?

Absolutely. His services are formularized from beginning to end. That's partly what I meant by saying that he was the beneficiary of all the ministries that have passed before him. He has not missed a thing. All of the best technique is at work here from the all-important planning and selection of the crusade to the actual offerings in the service itself. But let me tell you, it's not that easy. If it were all just formula, there would be hundreds of Benny Hinns running around. However, there is only one.

My conclusion? This is a genuine move of the Holy Spirit happening in our day, and it's still in its infancy. Anything can yet happen.

And yet there are many controversies.

Of course there are. As the French philosopher Rousseau said, "Everything changes, everything stays the same." The healing ministry was controversial in the time of Jesus, and it has never gotten any better. In fact, when confronted with irrefutable evidence of miracles, the religious leaders of Jesus' day concluded that it had all been done through the power of the devil.

In my opinion, any antipathy toward Benny Hinn's ministry comes from his television programming. Ironically, this is the one area where he does not follow the Kathryn Kuhlman formula. She interviewed guests, but she never showed excerpts from her services. Part of this was designed to keep the mystique that was a part of her style, and it is one of Benny Hinn's more dramatic departures from her. Hinn keeps nothing back. In his services, he talks almost out of stream of consciousness. But even more important than that, television is a very cool medium, as Kathryn Kuhlman knew so well, and healing services are hot. Some people think that they just don't come off well on television.

Now you've got me curious. Have you been to a Benny Hinn meeting? How are they different from what is shown on television?

I've slipped into his services, and they are wonderful. There is a very real and tender presence of the Holy Spirit. Nothing is contrived. Benny Hinn will wait hours if he has to until the audience finally gives up on the idea that he can do anything and turns its attention to God. It was a wonderful thing to experience. I had almost come to the conclusion that a new generation of Americans was going to miss the full power of the healing crusades that I had experienced. But I left feeling comforted that it is alive and well and in good hands. If you want a taste of what the revival was like in the 1950's, go to one of these crusades.

Television may not adequately capture it all. Believe me, if you've seen Benny Hinn on television, you have only seen a part of what his ministry is all about. For one thing, on television they go right to the healings, which is the most dramatic part. Yet in so doing they bypass all the tender worship. Of course, who would want to sit and watch that for hours on television?

How does the Benny Hinn story compare to all the others? Was there an alcoholic father? Did he have an early healing experience?

Like Oral Roberts and Kathryn Kuhlman, he had a stuttering problem. As far as that goes, so did Moses. Stuttering seems to be a prerequisite for a great ministry. Benny Hinn was born and raised in Jaffa, Israel. To this day he has many friends and contacts from those childhood years, a fact that really throws the American journalists who write about him. He has a pretty complex childhood. Basically, his family was Greek Orthodox, and yet little Benny was sent to a Catholic school. After the Six Day War Benny's parents decided that Israel was too hot and so emigrated to Canada. Sometime in the 1970's, he ended up on a chartered bus to a Kathryn Kuhlman service in Pittsburgh, and as they say, the rest is history.

I guess one thing that characterizes a Benny Hinn meeting is the large number of people who are "slain in the Spirit." He prays for them, and they just fall over. Sometimes it happens when he looks at them. It is much more pronounced than it was in Kathryn Kuhlman's ministry or William Branham's. And from what I am told, it is more pronounced than even in the Charles Price ministry. Some critics are asking if this is scriptural. They are suggesting that it is overdone.

The Bible says that "signs and wonders" will follow them that preach the gospel. I would categorize this phenomenon as a "wonder." Then, there is the moment when Jesus was confronted in the Garden of Gethsemane. He spoke to His accusers, and as He spoke they all fell down. There is the famous experience of Saul of Tarsus who was knocked down on the road to Damascus.

And yet, that seems like a very light scriptural rationale for such dramatics.

There are a lot of things that are in the Church that are useful and helpful that are not explicitly laid out in Scripture. Sunday school isn't there. Even more important, the altar call isn't there. Peter didn't stand up on the day of Pentecost and ask for a show of hands of those who wanted to accept Christ: "And now take the second step; stand to your feet. Now if you really mean it come down here and repeat the sinner's prayer after me." That whole tradition began with Charles Finney. It is not in the Bible. Most of the people whom you will meet in Heaven will have never even heard of an altar call. And yet it is not unscriptural, and it is, in fact, a useful device to bring someone to Christ and into baptism in water, which is the true, scriptural formula for salvation. The Bible says, "Those who believe and are baptized are saved, those who do not are damned" (see Mk. 16:16).

You said earlier that his ministry was still in its infancy, that anything could happen.

Yes, I believe that. If Benny Hinn just keeps on doing what he is doing now for another three years, he will go into the religious history books as one of America's greatest healing evangelists. But having said that, I wonder if his ministry will continue at the same pace for another three years. We live in a different time than that of the William Branham or Oral Roberts crusades. The media is more aggressive. The government is more intrusive and powerful. In my opinion, Benny Hinn will either explode on the national scene as a major public figure with his ministry at least partially vindicated, or he will be squashed. With his high-profile television ministry and with the flamboyant and controversial "falling under the power" openly shown, he will not remain untouched.

How does someone get squashed, especially if one is innocent?

Guilt or innocence has nothing to do with it. In fact, if he is innocent of any wrongdoing, it may even be more likely to happen. I would ask the opposite question that you are asking. I would ask, "How can the innocent avoid accusation?" In this very natural sense, Jesus Himself was squashed. He was misunderstood and lied about and eventually executed, although entirely innocent.

It could happen a hundred different ways. Maybe a person in a government agency who is very religious and who believes that Benny Hinn is in doctrinal error may decide that he has to be stopped. Someone may suspect that it is all a charade, that Benny is only an evangelist because he wants to enjoy a nice lifestyle, and pursue some type of inquest. As naive as that sounds to anyone in the ministry, the financial and lifestyle motivation is probably the predominant view of the secular world. In a ministry as big as Benny Hinn's, one with hundreds of employees, it is easy to find some disenchanted person who will feed you the information you want to hear. And if that happens, Benny Hinn's friends and denominational authorities will be likely to abandon him instantly. The press, which is hostile anyway, will make it too hot to go near him.

Have you been through this? Didn't A.A. Allen go through it as well?

In my case, there was a division in the board. Some wanted me to continue the process of carrying on A.A. Allen's ministry. Others now wanted to take it over for themselves. It turned out that some of the employees who actually designated where the money would be spent and who were responsible for keeping the documentation for each donation were themselves working with the new presumptive board. They spent money donated for one purpose on another, documented the whole thing, and then took it to the Attorney General's office as evidence that we were violating the law. Now how could I ever have protected myself from that? What could I have done differently? Thankfully, a very thorough investigation showed what had really happened, but if they had done just a few things a little bit differently, they would have gotten away with it and I would be sitting in jail somewhere. I would have been innocent, but only God and that new board would have known it or believed it. None of my brothers would have come to help.

Robert Tilton is a case in point. When the media hit him they took him down over the most ludicrous claims. A reporter stood in front of a trash container showing letters that had been sent into Tilton's office. This was supposed to show that Tilton really didn't care about the people's needs and that he had lied when he said that he prayed over their requests. According to the report, he had simply thrown out the mail.

The fact is, all such mail comes into professional caging operations where the personnel are bonded and the process is checked and doublechecked. They are usually not "in house" operations. The so-called news report was bogus, or at the best an aberration, a mistake by some employee.

The interesting thing was that the television network sent an undercover reporter to Tilton's meetings. She went down for healing, and when he touched her she fell over, cursing into her hidden microphone that "Wow, this guy has power."

One of America's most beloved national reporters covered the story, but after she got in her car to leave, her cameraman still had his camera going. Tilton's attorneys sued the television network and were given the tapes and other evidence. Apparently, the video just showed the floorboard of the automobile, but the audio was very clear. The reporter allegedly cursed and said something to the effect, "He hasn't done anything wrong, but he's perfect for our purposes. We will destroy him."

Tilton's attorneys sued of course, but what judge is going to rule against one of the top three American television networks? Tilton was all alone. And sadly, that's where Benny Hinn will be if it all falls apart on him. Innocence won't matter.

The public gets the impression that these ministries are rather loosely run affairs that benefit the evangelists. I can tell you that is not the case. Most of these ministries are under siege. Many have the very best accounting firms, and they have every sort of check and balance in place. Their books are open. They cannot afford to take chances, not in today's climate.

Benny Hinn was already the subject of a television attack. Allegations were made that he was making money off the ministry.

The big scandal was that he drove a Mercedes. Well, you may also have noticed that he sold his Mercedes and that the television program claimed a great victory in behalf of the people. It is all so laughable. The Mercedes was probably a better use of the Lord's money. It is all reminiscent of the television ministry that was criticized for having limousines. What the report didn't say was that the limousines had been donated. They hadn't cost the ministry a cent. But to avoid controversy, they had to sell the limousines and buy other automobiles at a net cost to the ministry of thousands of dollars. But in this case, Benny Hinn probably did the right thing by selling his Mercedes.

The news media has a very Catholic view of Christianity. They don't understand the doctrinal concept that God wants His people to be healthy, happy, and prosperous. They think that such teaching is only a gimmick, an excuse for the teacher to get rich. So we are all forced to accept the Catholic concepts that equate poverty with spiritual purity or else face the wrath of a self-righteous media. They are really very intolerant when it comes to religious doctrine.

My advice to Benny Hinn would be to keep his own spirit right. God has the power to protect him and keep him, even if there are challenges. But if he has the best lawyer and accountant in the world and lets his personal relationship with Christ wane, he could find himself in trouble. And then there is the other possibility. I believe that sometimes God allows some of His servants to experience their own Calvary to test the rest of us and to help us learn how to be dependent on Him.

The truth is, I don't expect any of that for Benny Hinn. I think that the more likely scenario is that his ministry will explode and be validated in some way. That could have easily happened in the Evander Holyfield case. It won't take too many more of such incidents to promote this ministry onto the national stage.

Help me out. What happened with Evander Holyfield?

Well, you know that Holyfield was the heavy weight boxing champion of the world. He lost his championship, and after his very next fight, he was pronounced unfit to ever box again. The examining doctors determined that he had a heart condition. His career was over.

Then Holyfield went to a Benny Hinn crusade. He described what felt like an electrical current running down through his body. Holyfield started telling everybody that he had been healed.

They wouldn't let him fight in Nevada, or New Jersey, or any of the other more regulated boxing states, but he found a place that would sanction a fight, and there was a large outcry. Anybody who watched ESPN or read the sports' pages during that time was well aware of the discussion. Commentators were outraged. Evander Holyfield was claiming that he had been healed and was going to have this fight, but the commentators thought that he would probably die because of it. They said that the whole idea was stupid and that he should not be allowed in the ring. They referred to it as barbaric. Boxing was in an uproar.

Evander Holyfield won his fight, doctors pronounced him fit and healthy, and he started on the comeback trail. Today, newspapers refer to Holyfield as having been "misdiagnosed" with a heart problem. They make no mention of the claim that he was healed. Interesting, huh?

Now that was a very public miracle that could have easily catapulted Benny Hinn onto the front pages. It didn't. But that is what I mean by saying that if he just keeps doing what he is doing for a few more years, it will explode nationally. You can't hold that sort of thing back. The healing ministry is that important to God. He isn't going to let it die out.

Why? The Bible says that "...it is appointed unto men once to die, but after this the judgment" (Heb. 9:27). In the light of eternity, what difference does it make if one person is blind for 70 years? Or even if one dies of cancer at the age of 50? What difference does it make?

I don't know the answer to that. Perhaps it is because God wants to demonstrate His love or mercy through a healing. Perhaps this too is a part of eternity, and how we live and feel matters to God. Maybe He feels that living with hope is better than living with fatalistic despair. Maybe He wants us to learn how to exercise and use our faith. Maybe He wants us to participate, to fight for our lives, instead of expecting Him to run everything by default. There must be something for us to learn in all of this. Maybe through seeking God for health, we draw closer to Him spiritually, which is what He really wants.

But He really heals people? You believe that? It is not all just psychological or misdiagnoses?

I know it. I've seen it. I've experienced it.

Let me tell you a story. Almost 40 years ago a young man named G.E. Mullenax walked into an A.A. Allen crusade in Little Rock, Arkansas. He was in bad shape. Doctors had removed three of his ribs and one lung, all apparently to get to a dead disc. He had almost died during the operation. He had laid on the operating table for five hours. During the procedure they had taken his heart out of its normal position and massaged it to keep him going. That was just unheard of in those days, and it was a very desperate thing to do. Afterward, they left a hole in his side about the size of a man's hand just to help with the drainage. It was not a good situation. It was very serious.

But he believed that God could heal him. A.A. Allen called him out of the crowd, listened to his story, showed the audience the hole in his side, and then prayed for him. Mullenax claimed an instantaneous healing. R.W. Shambach was there. Both he and Allen felt the place where the hole had been. Mullenax had a friend with him who ran up to the front and felt it too. Mullenax said that it felt like God had actually restored the ribs, which would have been a real miracle. The audience went wild. Mullenax just stood there weeping.

Of course, everybody wondered. Who is this guy? What happened to the hole in his side? They had all felt it. Or had they? Was his story true? Had doctors really removed the lung and ribs? And if so, why did it now feel like the ribs were restored? Had they instantaneously formed? Or had they been growing back ever since the operation?

Well, it turned out to be true. He came back nine days later with the doctor's X-rays and full reports. Allen wrote it up for *Miracle Magazine*.

Now there is a reason I'm telling you this particular story. Just a few months ago, almost 40 years after the fact, *The Pentecostal Evangel* reported the Mullenax miracle all over again. *The Pentecostal Evangel* is the voice of the Assemblies of God. This is the same denomination that had once dismissed and ridiculed A.A. Allen. One could say that this was a vindication for the evangelist. But the point is, the miracle was real and it is still real. After all these years, A.A. Allen is gone, but G.E. Mullenax is still with us.

Now let me ask you a question. How could a doctor misdiagnose the removal of a lung and ribs? Either they were taken out or they weren't. And how could the mind re-create a lung? The sets of X-rays show the whole story. They were gone, and now they are back. Explain that.

Now, you can still deny it, of course. Some refuse to even consider any evidence. Others say that it is all satanic, that the devil is doing all these wonderful things. Today we have a whole army of New Age experts. The generation before said that all those Bible stories were myths. Now, the New Age generation suddenly claims to be experts on how it all happens. Some say that it was aliens from other planets, or they may offer some new or more trendy, "designer" religion that explains everything while still letting them live the way that they want. But to anyone who really wants to know, Jesus is indeed the same yesterday, today, and forever. He is alive and well. He can touch you. Believe it.

All things are possible. Only believe.

Afterword

Only Believe. Simple, yet life-changing words. Jesus often used this admonition to challenge His disciples and others to enter the arena of the impossible boldly, and expect miracles to happen through the power of His name.

Only Believe. In Mark 5:36, Jesus comforted a fearful father's heart with these words, then proceeded to miraculously resurrect his daughter. Later, in Mark 9:23, Jesus challenged the doubting father of a demon-possessed son to "*believe,* [for] *all things are possible.*" Another miracle followed.

Only Believe. These words of Jesus were the touchstone for the great healing revival that swept across this nation and around the world. Some of my readers are old enough to remember the unique ministries that I've briefly described in these pages. Others are too young and so missed out on the unforgettable experiences of those powerful days.

It is my sincere prayer that as you were reading this book you were stirred by the stories of faith and daring that motivated great men of the past to phenomenal spiritual accomplishments. If you have been called to the ministry, I pray that God will give you direction and confidence to "covet earnestly the best gifts" and to inspire the fires of revival in your church and community. If you need healing today for a physical or emotional sickness, I pray that you have been challenged to let your faith soar and touch God for your personal healing.

My greatest objective is that a spiritual hunger will be created in your heart to believe for a revival...a renewal...a restoration of signs, wonders, and miracles.

We live in a time when the deceptions and counterfeits of the devil are more prevalent than I can ever remember. More and more people have turned to psychic mediums and fortune-tellers to find answers to their questions and problems. I believe the Church of Jesus Christ must shoulder the blame for the spiritual vacuum that forces hurting people to turn to demonic delusions for help. Now, more than ever, we must rise up as a united body of believers and revive the operation of all the gifts of the Spirit to tear down the strongholds of satan and defeat the forces of darkness.

I am not content with the blessings of the past. I am, however, eternally grateful and cherish all that God has allowed me to experience. My life and ministry are firmly founded on the claims of Hebrews 13:8: "Jesus Christ the same yesterday, and to day and for ever." I believe He can do it again...and best of all, He'll do it for you and me!

Could another great healing revival sweep across our nation? Is it possible that the pendulum could swing back once more and stir individuals and churches to demonstrate miracle power through the operation of the gifts of the Spirit?

"Only believe...all things are possible!" Jesus said it, and I believe it!

About the Author

Stricken with a crippling bone disease at the age of 13 and unable to walk without crutches after four major hip surgeries, Don Stewart received a miraculous healing. At that time, God called him to take His healing power to the nations of the world. For 40 years, Don Stewart has dedicated his life to the calling of healing human hurts, physically and spiritually. Preaching a dynamic message of power and mercy, Don has ministered to the sick and suffering in more than 75 nations of the world.

Don Stewart's message of God's power and mercy is based on his many years of evangelism experience. Discipled in the early 1960's by the beloved evangelist, A.A. Allen, Don preaches that God has something better than poverty, sickness, and defeat. Emphasizing restoration for the soul and body, Don's ministry is used by God to bring salvation, healing, and prosperity to multitudes throughout the world. He believes that, "If you have a need, you can have a miracle!"

The overriding theme of his message is "God wants to heal you everywhere you hurt." Respectfully called the "Evangelist of Compassion," he is touched and moved to action by the hurts and struggles of people. Don's message is simple with a prophetic anointing as he flows in the gifts of the Spirit, with special anointing for healing, miracles, and the word of knowledge.

Don Stewart is well-known for his emphasis on mass evangelism. Great citywide crusades are conducted in auditoriums, arenas, churches, and outdoor sites to reach vast crowds of hungry, searching souls with the gospel of power and mercy. He has conducted some of the largest religious services ever witnessed in Africa, South and Central America, the Philippines, and here in the United States, where he filled the world-famous Madison Square Garden in New York City, and thousands were saved and healed.

For information about Don Stewart conducting a crusade in your city or church, contact:

Field Department
Don Stewart Ministries
11052 N. 24th Avenue
Phoenix, AZ 85029
Telephone: 602-678-3280
Fax: 602-678-3288
E-mail: FMPIDSA@PrimeNet.com

Other *Destiny Image titles* you will enjoy reading

THE GOD CHASERS (Best-selling **Destiny Image** book)
by Tommy Tenney.
There are those so hungry, so desperate for His Presence, that they become consumed with finding Him. Their longing for Him moves them to do what they would otherwise never do: Chase God. But what does it really mean to chase God? Can He be "caught"? Is there an end to the thirsting of man's soul for Him? Meet Tommy Tenney—God chaser. Join him in his search for God. Follow him as he ignores the maze of religious tradition and finds himself, not chasing God, but to his utter amazement, caught by the One he had chased.
ISBN 0-7684-2016-4

GOD CHASERS DAILY MEDITATION & PERSONAL JOURNAL
by Tommy Tenney.
ISBN 0-7684-2040-7

ENCOUNTERING THE PRESENCE
by Colin Urquhart.
What is it about Jesus that, when we encounter Him, we are changed? When we encounter the Presence, we encounter the Truth, because Jesus is the Truth. Here Colin Urquhart, best-selling author and pastor in Sussex, England, explains how the Truth changes facts. Do you desire to become more like Jesus? The Truth will set you free!
ISBN 0-7684-2018-0

THE POWER OF BROKENNESS
by Don Nori.
Accepting Brokenness is a must for becoming a true vessel of the Lord, and is a stepping-stone to revival in our hearts, our homes, and our churches. Brokenness alone brings us to the wonderful revelation of how deep and great our Lord's mercy really is. Join this companion who leads us through the darkest of nights. Discover the *Power of Brokenness*.
ISBN 1-56043-178-4

AUDIENCE OF ONE
by Jeremy and Connie Sinnott.
More than just a book about worship, *Audience of One* will lead you into experiencing intimacy and love for the only One who matters—your heavenly Father. Worship leaders and associate pastors themselves, Jeremy and Connie Sinnott have been on a journey of discovering true spiritual worship for years. Then they found a whole new dimension to worship—its passion, intimacy, and love for the Father, your *audience of One*.
ISBN 0-7684-2014-8

Available at your local Christian bookstore.

Internet: http://www.reapernet.com

B6:59

Other
Destiny Image titles
you will enjoy reading

THE HIDDEN POWER OF PRAYER AND FASTING
by Mahesh Chavda.
How do you react when overwhelming defeat stares you in the eye? What do you do when faced with insurmountable odds? God has provided a way to turn certain defeat into awesome victory—through prayer and fasting! An international evangelist and the senior pastor of All Nations Church in Charlotte, North Carolina, Mahesh Chavda has seen firsthand the power of God released through a lifestyle of prayer and fasting. Here he shares from decades of personal experience and scriptural study principles and practical tips about fasting and praying. This book will inspire you to tap into God's power and change your life, your city, and your nation!
ISBN 0-7684-2017-2

THE KATHRYN KUHLMAN I KNEW
by Jimmie McDonald.
At first singer Jimmie McDonald was skeptical of Kathryn Kuhlman's healing ministry. But then he recognized the godly anointing that rested upon her. Drawing from his ministry experience with her, Jimmie goes beyond the glitz and glitter to show the real, down-to-earth side of the "Miracle Lady."
ISBN 1-56043-272-1

WHATEVER HAPPENED TO THE POWER OF GOD
by Dr. Michael L. Brown.
Why are the seriously ill seldom healed? Why do people fall in the Spirit yet remain unchanged? Why can believers speak in tongues and wage spiritual warfare without impacting society? This book confronts you with its life-changing answers.
ISBN 1-56043-042-7

EXTRAORDINARY POWER FOR ORDINARY CHRISTIANS
by Erik Tammaru.
Ordinary people don't think too much about extraordinary power. We think that this kind of power is for extraordinary people. We forget that it is this supernatural power that makes us all extraordinary! We are all special in His sight and we all have the hope of extraordinary living. His power can change ordinary lives into lives empowered by the Holy Spirit and directed by His personal love for us.
ISBN 1-56043-309-4

Available at your local Christian bookstore.

Internet: http://www.reapernet.com

Other
Destiny Image titles
you will enjoy reading

Other
*Destiny Image **titles***
you will enjoy reading

THIS GOSPEL OF THE KINGDOM
by Bertram Gaines.
What is your definition of the Kingdom of God? Some think that it's Heaven. Some think that it won't come until Jesus does. But Jesus said the Kingdom of God would come with power before all His disciples passed away! Here Bertram Gaines, teacher of the Kingdom Life Bible Seminars and a pastor, explains that the Kingdom of God is a spiritual system of righteous government. It's available to believers today, and God wants you to have a part in it!
ISBN 1-56043-323-X

FAITH WORKS
by R. Russell Bixler.
The story of Russ and Norma Bixler's pioneering work in Christian television for Pittsburgh is a testimony to the power of faith in God! From a tiny trailer on a hilltop to a massive earth station and satellite uplink, Cornerstone TeleVision has touched multitudes of lives with the good news and healing power of Jesus Christ. This book will encourage you to pursue God's call on your life no matter what obstacle you face!
ISBN 1-56043-338-8

MOMMA, WHAT'S IT LIKE TO DIE?
by Myrna L. Etheridge.
How do you cope with daily life when your children are born with a genetic illness? How do you deal with the loss when young lives are cut tragically short? Meet Myrna Etheridge, a mother and teacher whose life was radically changed by the deaths of her two young sons as a result of cystic fibrosis. Follow Myrna as she travels through mourning into victory, from sadness into joy, and once again finds love and peace. Let her discoveries of God's grace and healing power transform your life!
ISBN 1-56043-331-0

WHEN GOD STRIKES THE MATCH
by Dr. Harvey R. Brown, Jr.
A noted preacher, college administrator, and father of an "all-American" family—what more could a man want? But when God struck the match that set Harvey Brown ablaze, it ignited a passion for holiness and renewal in his heart that led him into a head-on encounter with the consuming fire of God.
ISBN 0-7684-1000-2

Available at your local Christian bookstore.

Internet: http://www.reapernet.com